JAIL TALES

By

Chris Duffin

Aided and Abetted
by Harry Duffin

To Yvonne,
With best wishes
Chris Duff

JAIL TALES

Cumulus Publishing Limited
9 Broadway Street
Martinborough
Wairarapa 5711
New Zealand

Please note that this publication is based on the author's personal experience and anecdotal evidence. I have tried to recreate events, locales and conversations from my memories of them.
I have made every reasonable attempt to achieve complete accuracy of the content, but in order to maintain their anonymity in some instances I may have changed some identifying characteristics and details. This publication is a creative work copyrighted by the author and fully protected by all applicable copyright laws.

ISBN 978-0-473-19939-5

I would like to dedicate this book to all the quirky, unconventional yet dedicated Governors and staff I had the pleasure of working with during my time in the Prison Service.

Chris Duffin

October 2011

PREFACE

Ever since I joined the Prison Service in 1978 I have regaled friends and relatives with some of the many incidents and stories I experienced behind bars. I have lost count of the number of times I have been told "you should write a book".

Well, at long last, here it is.

It's not a blow-by-blow account of my long career, or a history of the service I was proud to serve for many years. These are just a collection of 'jail tales' meant to entertain over a nice glass of wine.

Over the years some people have not believed some of my stories and many other members of staff have stories (they tell me) much better than mine. These are my own recollections and some people may have different memories of the same events. But, as someone once said, why let a fact get in the way of a good story?

Harry and I have had a great deal of fun writing this book and I hope you have as much fun reading it.

We would like to add a grateful 'Thanks' to Rod Davis, Joe Hinch and Adam and Raymond Thompson for their invaluable help and support.

PROLOGUE

'I am by nature shy, quiet and retiring.'

So there I was, rookie prisoner officer Christine Zapletal, standing in the doorway of a prison house at Styal Women's Prison, waiting for 'my' twenty-odd girls to leave for their days work around the jail. In those days the houses at Styal were all named after prison reformers, Fry House, Howard House, etc and, as luck would have it, mine was named after a certain John Hooker. And where had the powers that be decided to put all the prostitutes? In a house with a large sign above the door reading 'HOOKER'. Beneath which it was my job to stand every morning.

Each day the girls filed out with comments like, 'Getting much business, Miss?'

To which I replied, 'No. Too many amateurs in here giving it away. We've got to organize and get our prices right, ladies.'

On reflection, I think I'd always wanted to be a professional screw. I just couldn't decide whether or not to wear a uniform.

CHAPTER ONE

'Abandon Hope'

Even in glorious summer sunshine Dartmoor Prison looks grim and unwelcoming. So driving up to the forbidding gateway through grey April drizzle conjured up thoughts of gruesome horrors enacted by escaped convicts on the surrounding moors. My ancient car being, once again, given the kiss of life by my friendly mechanic, I had been driven for my prison service enrolment exam by a friend, her husband, and their young children.

As we pulled up, her husband said, 'Here we are,' with the air of a judge donning his black cap. 'Abandon hope all ye who enter here!' (I was to find out later that those exact words were above the reception at Strangeways Prison, Manchester.)

My friend punched his shoulder and shot an embarrassed glance at me seated with the two children in the back seat.

I gathered my handbag, regretting I hadn't thought to bring an umbrella. After all it had been brilliant spring sunshine in the valley a mile below. Years later I was to learn this was typical of Dartmoor and Princetown, the little village where the prison stood. Sunshine, rain, snow and fog all in one day. 'Tis normal, me handsome,' as the locals say.

Reaching for the door handle I felt a little hand tug at my sleeve. 'Don't go in there, Auntie Chris!' pleaded a tiny voice. 'There's lots of bad men in there. They might not let you out again!'

She had a point. Out of the mouths of babes, etc. What did I know about what went on behind those gloomy, granite walls? And what was I doing at thirty years old, applying to join Her Majesty's Prison Service?

Well, firstly, the Tamar Dam had recently been completed so my contract as secretary to the chief engineer had come to an end. (As far as I'm aware, I'm still the only prison governor, past or present, able to calculate the standard deviation for the pouring of ready-mixed concrete. Should any of you urgently need to know.)

Second, after giving birth to two still-born babies, my first marriage had collapsed, there were money problems and I needed a job.

As a teenager back home in Manchester I had applied to join the Cheshire police force as a cadet, but by the time they got round to writing to say I'd been accepted I had found another job which I enjoyed, so my embryonic career as Inspector Jane Tennison never got off the ground. ('Prime Suspect' remember?) Now keen to resurrect it I called the Devon and Cornwall Police where, to my delight, a nice woman informed me that I seemed an ideal candidate. And how old was I? On learning that I had attained the ripe old age of thirty, she said that, sadly, I was too old. Too old at thirty! My career prospects looked bleak.

Since starting work at sixteen I had never been out of a job, so it was a humbling and daunting experience having to join the queue at the labour exchange to sign on the dole. Standing waiting my turn in the long, glum queue I noticed a stack of leaflets entitled 'Join the Modern Prison Service'. Not knowing a modern prison service from an old-fashioned one, I picked up a leaflet and with true vocational spirit turned to the back to find out at what age the prison service considered me to be on the scrap heap. Learning that I would be accepted up to age forty-two and a half (forty-five if I was ex-armed forces) straight away I decided that this was an organization that truly deserved me. So here I was, several weeks later, standing dripping before the gates of Dartmoor awaiting my fate.

A small hatch opened in the main gate at my tentative knock

and a male face beneath a shiny peaked cap peered suspiciously at me. Deciding that I wasn't a mad axe murderer, (well they had their fair share of them in there already) a larger door opened and I stepped inside, just as the sun broke out.

Was this an omen, or just the vagaries of Dartmoor weather? 'Tis normal, me handsome!'

'Underline the correct word' was the instruction on the exam paper. 'I .... walking down the street.'

(a) were (b) was (c) is.

I stared at the paper perplexed. This was the tenth blindingly simple question in a row. The two young children, waiting in the nearby pub with their parents, could have sailed through the exam. Surely this was some kind of trick? What was I missing?

Nothing as it turned out. The Principal Officer administering the test informed me that I was the first one hundred per cent student he had ever had! God knows, I thought, I'm not Mensa material so what are the rest like?

As Dartmoor was, at that time, an all male-staffed prison there was no one able to give me my medical. So while the other male candidates were prodded, poked and coughing, I was shown around the extensive grounds by the Principal Officer (henceforth to be called P.O's, so pay attention).

Dartmoor, he informed me, was built by French prisoners from the Napoleonic wars, and was the only circular prison in the country. 'We used to have armed guards on horseback, patrolling the outside wall,' he said proudly. 'Not anymore though,' he sighed, lamenting the demise of the custodial John Waynes.

'Times are changing,' he said. 'I wouldn't be surprised if one day you came back here as my boss.'

Ten years later he was waiting at the main gates to greet me when I arrived as the new governor 3rd in charge. 'What did I tell you, governor?' he said with a grin...I nearly fell out of my saddle.

Sorry, I'm getting ahead of myself. Several weeks after I took the exam two letters arrived by the same post. The first asking me to report to Exeter prison for my interview. (I had passed the entrance exam, the next step was an interview.) The second was from my doctor informing me that I was pregnant for the third time. Great timing... After arranging for a postponed interview, I spent the next twenty-odd weeks flat on my back in a hospital bed for 'bed-rest'. When the third baby died, I took it as a sign. Fate didn't want me to be a mother. It had other plans.

CHAPTER TWO

'The Spice Girls'

Florene was tall, black and gorgeous. (Still is.) We met during our four week stint shadowing officers at Styal Womens' Prison before starting our basic training, and we hit it off immediately.

Unlike the prison officers, we trainees wore civilian clothes and didn't carry keys. So, as there were no black women in the prison service at that time Flo was regularly mistaken for a prisoner, and staff kept trying to lock her up. We laughed about it, but sadly the stereotype `black equals criminal' still prevails in some quarters.

Flo shared her beloved Ford Capri with her brother, so early one Monday morning I picked her up to drive to Wakefield to start our training. Whether through devilment, or maybe it was just too early in the morning, I decided to swing back home to say 'Goodbye' to my mother.

Born just before the Great War in cosy, working-class Ashton-under-Lyne like most of her generation my mother was prejudiced. Being a strict God-fearing lay preacher she was doubly prejudiced.

We waltzed in the front door to be confronted by a vision in pink. My mother halfway down the stairs, in dressing gown, hairnet and slippers, minus her false teeth. Now in those days black people in Ashton were as rare as hens' teeth, so to have one in your hallway at seven in the morning was a huge shock. So much so that my mother's jaw dropped wide open before she remembered and clamped both hands over the gaping gummed cavern.

Flo sized up the situation immediately. 'It's alright, Mrs Roberts,' she beamed, by way of contrast showing her full set of gleaming white teeth. 'I'll go and make you a nice cup of tea. Kitchen this way is it?' And vanished down the tiny hall to the kitchen.

My mother stood frozen on the stairs. Not only a black woman in her house before sunrise, but in her kitchen. Making tea! I saw her brain racing. What would she say to the neighbours? Could she show her face in the corner shop again? Would she still be allowed to preach at Sunday School? Would she be drummed out of the amateur dramatic society? (Not likely as she ran it, with a rod of iron.)

It was the first of several culture shocks my poor mother had to endure due to my joining Her Majesty's Prison Service.

Despite the age gap, Flo and I have many things in common. Top of the list a deep and profound love of spicy food. Born in the Leeward Islands and winding up in the North of England, Flo found that the only way she could get food with a real kick was by cooking it herself at home. (She is a brilliant cook.)

Not being at home Flo's taste buds were pining. College canteen bangers, mash and gravy just didn't do it, and she was almost ready to throw up her career to go back to Manchester to rustle up a Caribbean gumbo. Way before chicken tikka masala became Britain's favourite dish such food was hard to come by, especially 'Up North' in Wakefield. So at night we scoured the surrounding Pennines searching for the sort of tiny restaurant that you could smell even before you could see it. A fiery jewel nestled behind a brooding granite crag, hiding from the culinary wrath of the hard, no-nonsense gentlefolk of Wakefield and vicinity. But with no luck. Flo was getting desperate.

Rescue came in the form of my two American friends staying in Harrogate, who invited us over for dinner. For those of you who have never been there, though much further 'Up North' than Wakefield, Harrogate restaurateurs consider themselves the pride of the Home Counties. And consequently, on occasion, have been known to omit the gravy and serve spicy food.

For starters – garlic snails! For main course, garlic snails. Desert? Garlic snails with ice-cream. We thought we'd died and gone to heaven.

The classroom was full of bleary-eyed students as Flo and I walked in at eight-thirty the next morning. Now the odd whiff of garlic may not have been unknown among the Seventies Hampstead set, but 'Up North' in Wakefield, hitherto, garlic had only been used by witches, or for warding off vampires. It wasn't something you cooked with. Let alone ate in copious quantities.

'By Christ! What's that fucking smell!' was the general consensus of the now wide-awake students.

Flo and I looked around, puzzled. Everyone was staring at us. One of the brilliant qualities of garlic is that if everyone has eaten it no one can smell it. But if you are the only two in a tiny classroom of twenty...When we returned from grabbing a coffee before the class began it was to find our two desks placed firmly out in the corridor. An early example of the kind of initiative trainee prison officers need to show to survive.

CHAPTER THREE
'When "trannies" meant radios.'

It's a long-standing tradition that every jail has its resident cartoonist. Often they are figures of mystery, like the Scarlet Pimpernel, unknown, sought but seldom caught, as they post their scurrilous and hilarious drawings around the jail to embarrass both staff and inmates alike.

Wakefield Prison College where I did my basic training was no exception. Unfortunately for trainee officer Rennie.

After classes, being a lusty lad, Officer Rennie was wont to repair to town with his mates to sample what passed for nightlife in 1970's Wakefield. At that time it was still a mining town, fanatical about rugby league, full of hard, no-nonsense men, and equally hard, no-nonsense women.

Having consumed copious amounts of Samuel Smith's best, (a secret unknown to anyone South of Watford), the boys found themselves late at night in a steamy, dimly-lit nightclub. Handsome young Rennie was immediately hit on by a gorgeous, voluptuous blonde, who promptly covered his face with passionate kisses. Unable to believe his luck and anxious to capitalize on it before the woman changed her mind, or he fell over, Rennie rushed his new lady-love into the darkened car-park.

Bending his more-than-willing lover backwards over the spacious bonnet of a Volvo, he thrust his hand, in a no-nonsense fashion, straight up her mini-skirt, between her solid, no-nonsense thighs and copped a generous handful of what is called in polite circles 'meat and two veg.'

Unknown to the prison college students, even in the Seventies, Wakefield also had a core of hard, no-nonsense transvestites, and they had stumbled into the most infamous 'gender-bender' club within a hundred mile radius (not counting Doncaster, but that's another story).

Having made his excuses and staggered away into the night, shocked and horrified, as any young, hot-bloodied lad would be, Rennie made one final, crucial mistake. He told his mates...

The cartoon posted on the notice board the next morning depicted a scene of Hogarthian debauchery featuring a young, trainee prison officer, hat askew and disheveled, bending wide-eyed and open-mouthed over a gorgeous woman draped across the bonnet of a top of the range Swedish saloon, with his hand firmly up the mini-skirt, clutching his partner's finely delineated cock and balls. (Michaelangelo would have been envious.) The caption read – 'Feeling queer? Suck a Rennie!'

A valuable lesson learnt for any would-be prison officer – Never trust anyone. Especially not your mates.

CHAPTER FOUR
'Chiefs and Indians'

Before the rank was abolished in the 1980's Chief Officers had ruled the roost in British jails since God's planning committee rejected Noah's initial plans for the Ark. Usually recruited from the military, the majority of male Chiefs were staunch members of the 'funny handshake' brigade and knew all too well how to look after their own.

Chiefs were the spiders at the centre of each prison web. They controlled the uniformed officers who ran the prison day to day and so generally believed that they, not the governing governor, were the true 'A Number One, King of the Hill, Top of the Heap.' (I'm writing this having just been to New York and Frank's phrase just popped into my head.) Even governors, technically higher in rank, had to tread carefully around the Chief if they wanted a quiet life. Or any life at all. And woe betide any probationary officer who fell foul of them, as I discovered in my first posting back at Styal prison.

I don't know what I did to upset her. Maybe it was because I took elocution and deportment instead of Latin at Fairfield High School for Girls, and could write an incident report in grammatical English. Whatever it was the Chief 'took agin me'. (It can't just have been because I could walk across a room balancing a book on my head, can it?)

Shortly after I started at Styal my cousin, Janet, had a baby. Very thoughtfully, knowing I'd lost three babies of my own, she asked me to attend the christening to act as godmother to her daughter. I was touched and delighted. Having arranged it with Flo I put in a request to swap shifts with her so I could be at the christening. It was a normal request and usually granted without a murmur. But even though she knew the circumstances behind the request, the Chief refused it.

'You don't have a private life when you become a prison officer,' she told me. Which was bollocks, of course, because I knew that lots of shift-swapping went on among the rest of the staff.

So I applied for leave for that day. Refused. Sensing an injustice I appealed to the regional office for a ruling, as I was entitled to. On my next shift I was summoned before the Chief.

She was livid that I had questioned her decision and gone over her head. Apparently no one ever had. She picked up a small orange book and shook it in my face. 'Read the staff hand book! Leave is a privilege not a right!'

Calmly as I could, (I was actually shaking inside because this woman held my career in her hands), I told her that I had read the book before I made the appeal and that I could see no grounds for her refusal.

Her face turned puce. Flinging back her arm, she hurled the book with all her might straight at me yelling, 'Knowledge is power!'

In those days I was younger and fitter and played netball three times a week. I ducked as the book flew past my head. It bounced off the door and landed at my feet.

Bending down I picked up the book and calmly placed it on her desk. Where the next words came from I'll never know but without a pause I said, 'And megalomania is a very serious disease, for which the only cure is humble pie to be eaten three times a day.'

As I walked out, I heard the 'thud' of the book hitting the door again. I won the appeal. The christening was a wonderful occasion. But I'd made a powerful enemy and knew I had to watch my back from now on.

Prison officers can be dismissed for any number of misdemeanors. The most heinous crime, naturally, is failing to lock doors. I mean, fair do's, this is a prison we're talking about. Its main function is to keep people locked up, after all. I have no quarrel with that. If you wander about with a bunch of keys jangling on your belt as a constant reminder to lock doors and then leave them wide open so rapists and murderers and Ernest Saunders can walk out... (Hang on! He was released on medical grounds. Then miraculously recovered. The only known case in medical science of someone recovering from Alzheimer's.) But you get my drift. If you screw up, big style, you deserve all you get. Which in most cases is fairly instant dismissal.

Now officers and prisoners are supposed to be on different sides. That's the general public perception. But, first and foremost, prisoners are human beings like the rest of us. They can be bad or good. Mean or kind. Spiteful or generous. And without one such act of generosity I wouldn't be sitting trying to write this book. I don't know what I'd be doing but it wouldn't be talking about my life as a prison governor.

One day, having finished my shift and handed in my keys at the centre, I was (were, is) walking to the main gate when I heard a frantic knocking coming from nearby Hooker House, the house I was in charge of. A prisoner, Jean, the cook for the house, was banging on the kitchen window and gesticulating wildly towards the front door. Knowing I'd locked the gate, I still decided to retrieve my keys and investigate. The gate had been unlocked. I discovered later by a P.O. who was thick as thieves with the chief. Bless you, Jean, wherever you are.

CHAPTER FIVE
'I just want to pay my taxes!'

'I can't bloody believe it! I just find a punter who makes me the easiest money I've ever made and then I get nicked! By the time I get out some other bugger will have snapped him up!'

It was a wet Saturday afternoon in Styal. On such days, when I was on duty, I used to sit around the fire with some of the inmates and listen to their stories about life 'on the game'. A lot of the women, (some of them still girls, really) were single mums who turned to prostitution to feed their kids and/or their drug habit. Their stories were often weird, always entertaining. This has to be one of the most bizarre I heard.

The story-teller had been contacted by the man and arranged to meet him in a hotel. When she arrived he asked her to leave her handbag on the bed, go into the bathroom, lock the door, then strip naked, calling out all the time through the closed door what she was doing. She did that and was standing stark naked in the bathroom, wondering what was going to happen next, when she heard the door open and close. Immediately, her heart began to race.

'Oh, no,' she thought, 'he's let a mate in.' What were they going to do to her? She'd heard many stories of girls being beaten and much worse. She waited, holding her breath, cold and frightened. She waited. And waited. And waited...At last, unable to contain her curiosity, she got dressed, opened the bathroom door and peered out. The room was empty. And on the bedside table was the money.

'I thought, weird, but hey, thank you very much!'

Picking up her handbag, she smelt a foul smell. Opening it, she discovered that the man had left a calling card inside. 'He'd only gone and had a dump in me bag, hadn't he?!'

A week later the man contacted her again. Same routine. Only this time she had the foresight to pop into a charity shop and buy a second-hand bag for a couple of bob. 'No point ruining me Louis Vuitton knockoff, was there?' And, clever girl, she didn't even bother to get undressed. She just called out from the bathroom what she was 'not' doing while she sat on the loo and filed her nails. And the money was there again.

'He used to call me once or twice a week. The charity shop did alright, and for me it was money for jam..well, you know what I mean. Christ knows what he did for a shit the rest of the week!'

Another time two young women arrived in a hotel room to find the punter standing beside an open coffin. 'We thought, fuck, this doesn't look too good!'

But the man simply instructed one girl to don a shroud and lie in the coffin, arms crossed, eyes closed, while the other, dressed as a choirboy, stood at the end reading from a prayer book. The man himself just stood at the head of the coffin masturbating until he came over the 'dead' woman. Then he calmly thanked them, paid them the money and they left. 'What the hell was going through that poor fucker's head is anybody's guess!'

The women had many stories. All revealing the bizarre and secret underside of British society. From bankers to bakers; politicians to postmen; judges to jurymen. The Sun newspaper doesn't know the half of it. Or if it does it's too scared to print it in case it gets sued, again.

'What I can't understand, Mrs Z...' With a name like Zapletal I got called all kind of strange names. Zabaglionni, Zabbatini, Zappetally, and even Zatopek. To which, of course, I replied 'I can't run that fast.' Finally all the inmates settled on 'Mrs Z' as being the easiest. Except one newcomer who asked what she should call me, and when I said, 'Mrs Z'll do,' she replied brightly 'Alright, Mrs Zedaldo.' And 'Mrs Zedaldo' I stayed for her. It was a bit of a relief when I remarried some years later and became Mrs Ellis. Even though that was, unfortunately, the surname of the last woman in Britain to be hanged.

'What I can't understand, Mrs Z, is why we keep getting arrested. I mean, what are we doing that's wrong? We advertise a service, we perform it and we get paid. Just like any other business. And we help the poor buggers who can't get it any other way. Cripples and poor sods like that. And we deal with the weirdos. Helps keeps the streets safe for ordinary women, dun't it?'

You'll get no argument from me. Other countries have legalized brothels which pay business rates and taxes on their net profit. Their prostitutes are registered, have regular health checks and pay income tax. In Britain we fine women for soliciting. So they have to go back on the streets in order to pay the fine. Then they're arrested again and fined until, when finally they can't pay the fine, the state slams them in prison and, not only has to house and feed them, but also has to pay to put their children in care. Helping to destroy a family and create even more disaffected kids for society to deal with later down the line.

'I'm a businesswoman, Mrs Z. I just want to pay my taxes!'

It was an argument I'd heard many times. We have a completely crazy system, if they ask me. But they never have.

CHAPTER SIX

'Don't mention the war!'

Thankfully fashions change. Probably as a throwback to the British military tradition both male and female prison staff not only had to wear uniforms, which is pretty sensible when you think about it, (don't want to be clobbering one of your own in a riot), but also hats, which is pretty stupid as hats are the first thing to get knocked off in said riot.

When I joined the prison service, along with an impractical pillbox hat, the uniform also included a knee-length TIGHT skirt. (You heard me). Imagine, if you will, when the alarm bell rings, the sight of half a dozen female officers racing to the incident hanging onto their hats and hitching their skirts up their thighs so they can actually run. It helped to quell riots though as the prisoners cracked up when they saw us hobbling towards them like a scene from the Keystone Cops.

But hats were mandatory as I found out when reporting for one winter morning shift. Unknown to me, on arriving home from work the previous night, I had dropped my hat on the drive in my hurry to get from the car and into the house before I contracted frostbite. (Winters can be cold 'Up North'.) Rushing to the car next morning I stood on the hat, picked it up and threw it on the passenger seat. As the car heater began to take effect so did the smell emanating from my squashed hat. Whatever animal had relieved itself inside was very, very poorly. Throwing the hat in the boot, I drove on and arrived just in time to collect my keys and line up for the daily inspection.

The inspecting P.O. strutted along the line of officers and stopped in front of me. 'Ver is your hat?', she barked. (She was German).

In my best Frank Spencer voice I replied, 'The cat did a whoopsee in it.' Everyone laughed but the P.O. (She was German).

'You vill get a hat before you finish your shift,' she said sternly. 'You vill not be allowed to leave zee prison improperly dressed.'

I felt like I was back in the Fairfield High School for Girls. But more important where could I get a hat on a Sunday when the staff stores were closed? The prospect of spending all night in the nick waiting for the stores to open on Monday morning wasn't very appealing. And my new partner would be waiting for his dinner.

A prisoner in my unit heard about my predicament on the grapevine. (There are no secrets in prisons.)

'I hear a cat shat in your hat,' she said

'Thanks for the sympathy,' I replied.

'It's not a problem, Mrs Z. Mrs Carpenter keeps a spare hat in her locker.'

'Great. But I don't have her key,' I explained, as if to a three-year old.

'But I have a hairgrip,' she replied, as if to a cretin.

Before I drove home at the end of the shift, I phoned Mrs Carpenter and explained why I had borrowed her hat for the day. She was quite happy about it, but the P.O. wasn't.

Yet another inmate with a heart of gold and life skills I could only dream of.

'Do you speak German, miss?', a young inmate, May, asked me one day. She explained that her grandmother lived in Germany and wrote letters to her in German. 'I want to write back to her in German, but I don't know how to say this sentence.'

'I don't speak much,' I replied, staring at the sentence which was way beyond my feeble grasp of the Teutonic tongue.

At that moment May saw the P.O. with the hat fetish walking past the window. 'She does, Miss. I wonder if she would help?

I knew the P.O. was going down to the punishment block so I rang and asked to speak to her.

Her dulcet voice came on the line. 'Vat do you vant?'

I told her that May wanted help with writing a letter to her grandmother in German and she wondered if she could help. Her reply was priceless.

'How does she know zat I am German?! Prisoners are not supposed to know anythink about ze staff. How does she know zat I am German?'

'People talk,' I replied.

One of the duties of a P.O. was to supervise the vetting of mail in and out of the prison. Valuable information about what is going on among the prisoners, who is bullying who, etc, can often by found in an unguarded letter.

Flo and I were on duty together when our Germanic P.O. approached brandishing an envelope.

'Does either of you speak French?' she asked.

I said that I did a little.

'Good,' she said. 'I want you to look at ziz French letter.'

As Flo and I struggled to keep a straight face, I replied, 'I hope it's not used.'

She didn't get it. (Did I mention she was German?)

CHAPTER SEVEN

'Two old ladies locked in the...'

Before I joined the prison service, if I ever thought about it at all, I suppose I had the widely-held, knee-jerk view that prisoners 'got what they deserved.' I'd never knowingly met a criminal, (though some businessmen I worked for sailed close to the wind,) so I was as ignorant as the 'Man on the Clapham Omnibus.' (Of which more later.)

Soon after becoming a rookie screw I learnt that prisoners come in all shapes and sizes, from all walks of life, and that you should 'never judge a book by its cover.'

That was demonstrated to me dramatically in the form of a little old lady who I had to escort from the 'lifer' unit to the medical wing to take her regular tablets. (You can't just dole out tablets to prisoners because other prisoners would steal them. Anything is currency in prison.) She was a frail old dear in her late seventies who had, some time ago, suffered a stroke which left part of her face paralysed.

We chatted as I helped her along, about her grandkids and so on, and she seemed just like the nice old lady who ran the corner shop when I was a girl. When we got back to her unit I asked the officer in charge what such a sweet old lady was doing in the lifer unit? Maybe I felt deep down that there must have been a miscarriage of justice. (It happens more than you'd believe.)

'Sweet?!' was the reply. And then I was told the story.

Apparently, my 'nice old lady' had been unluckily married three times, as one by one her husbands left her. She lived on in her home for many years as neighbours grew more and more suspicious, until eventually someone grassed her up to the police.

On searching the house the police found a plastered patch down in the cellar which had clearly been done by an amateur. As they broke through the plaster out tumbled three bodies in various states of decomposition. The corpses of her three unfortunate, murdered husbands.

At which point the 'sweet' old lady had a stroke.

Sometime later, while serving as assistant governor at HMP Strangeways, I was temporarily posted as governor in charge to Drake Hall women's open prison. The governor there had health problems and I was told by regional office that I would be spending 'a couple of weeks in the country.' Ten months later...

In one of the units, which were largely filled with young girls and women convicted of petty offences like shop-lifting, there was a seventy-six year old woman who had been given fourteen days for non-payment of rates, (I think it was.)

Having lived on her own for many years, after the legitimate death of her husband, the old lady found that she really enjoyed the company of the lively young females. And, as a lot of the girls came from poor, inadequate homes and families, where caring women role models were unknown, the older woman quickly became a 'granny' figure to them. She taught them skills hitherto unknown to them, ancient, archaic skills like knitting and sewing and darning. And she enjoyed helping them out in the gardens, which the women tended very conscientiously. (The majority of them coming from tower block estates had never seen a garden.)

One day, before the woman had served her time, her son arrived at the prison gates asking to see the governor. He told me that he wanted to pay his mother's fine, which meant that she would be free to go immediately. On being told the news, instead of being relieved, the woman replied that she was enjoying herself and didn't want to go. What did she have to go back to anyway?

But her son insisted. And as the governor, despite her protests, I was not allowed to refuse the payment of the fine. So against her wishes the old woman had to pack up her 'parrots and monkeys' and leave. (No, she didn't actually *have* any parrots and monkeys, it's just an old nautical expression.) On leaving she vowed that she wouldn't pay her rates again and so would get a longer sentence next time. I bet she kept her word.

A footnote. By Spring the next year a new, permanent governor had been appointed for Drake Hall and I had returned to Strangeways. Though I don't think this had anything to do with the old lady, I am told that when the crocuses poked their heads from the green lawns in front of the prison their petals brightly spelt out the word 'Bollocks'.

At least I don't think it had anything to do with the old lady...

CHAPTER EIGHT

'Walk a mile in my ballet shoes'

While on basic training at Wakefield a tutor suggested that I should sit the exam for accelerated promotion to governor grade. (In those days there were five governor grades, five being the lowest.) On the day of the exam as the only other option was a cross country run in the rain it was a no brainer. I opted for the dry exam room, sat the exam and thought no more about it.

As luck would have it I was actually on sick leave from Styal, recovering from an appendicitis op, when a letter came telling me I had passed the exam and to report to Wakefield College for an follow-up interview. It was lucky because if I had been on duty the Chief would probably have made it difficult for me to get leave to go.

So by the time I returned to work at Styal I had learnt that, as soon as the next intake of governors was due, I would be given a posting as assistant governor. And the Chief had heard the news too.

Though she was many things, the Chief wasn't stupid and knew the expression 'be kind to those beneath you on the ladder in case you meet them again on your way down.' I actually prefer the old Chinese proverb, 'Build golden bridges over which your enemy can retreat.' If only some of our rulers had practiced that I think the world would be a much safer place. (Are you listening George and Tony?)

Anyway the result was that the change of attitude of the Chief and my 'favourite' P.O made the rest of my time at Styal much easier.

Stoke Heath, where I was posted in my first role as probationary assistant governor, was a Borstal. They were places where naughty boys, under the age of eighteen, were sent to learn from other naughty boys how to become naughtier. Though in some cases that didn't work and they actually improved.

One shining success was 024 Jones. (Being close to Wales Stoke

Heath had a lot of Joneses.) Like many of his fellow prisoners, it's fair to say that Jones had not had the best start in life. With an absentee father, his mother turned to prostitution to feed her son and consequently spent a lot of time in prison. So 024 Jones's childhood had been a succession of care homes and foster parents and, when we first met, he was not a happy bunny.

His insolent, disruptive attitude to authority had severely pissed off some of the male staff, so when I suggested that giving him some responsibility might help there was universal disbelief. (The male staff resented taking orders from a female anyway, but more of that later.)

When I told Jones that I was appointing him as teaboy he was as gobsmacked as the staff. In fact at first he refused and had to be persuaded, and only then agreed on a two week trial basis. As teaboy 024 Jones proved a resounding success. Having some status for the first time in his life, he blossomed.

So when we needed some help laying a patio at home 024 Jones was an obvious choice. As a matter of fact we didn't really need the help as my new husband was a builder but, prior to release, spending time outside and doing a job was seen as part of the rehabilitation process for young offenders.

That Sunday as Jones and another inmate helped with the patio, I cooked our usual roast beef and Yorkshire pudding, with all the trimmings. When it was time to eat the other lad went into the downstairs bathroom to wash his hands and Jones stood at the bottom of the stairs not moving. I told him there was a bathroom upstairs where he could wash his hands.

He looked at me surprised and said, 'You trust me to go up there on my own?' It turns out that when you haven't been anywhere on your own unescorted for years it's a hard habit to break.

Later, seated at the table with my family, Jones sat staring at his untouched food for a while and then quietly asked to be excused. My husband told me afterwards that when he followed Jones into the lounge he found the boy in tears. Jones confessed to him that he had never in his life sat down to a family meal before and would find it hard to swallow the food. When I heard that I shed a tear too.

In the afternoon the sky grew gloomy and the rain came down. So, as no work could be done on the patio, Jones spent the time happily teaching my three adopted kids how to cheat at cards. It was a lovely family scene and I like to think that for the first time he felt connected.

Later that year, after his release, Jones came to Stoke Heath to see me, tanned and beaming. He told me that he had spent the summer working as a life guard, and now had a permanent job. For years afterwards, until I was moved around so much that sometimes even I lost track of where I lived, Jones sent me a card at Christmas telling me he was doing well. I hope he's having a great life. After the start he had he deserves it.

You may not believe this but, in my day, pink jump suits were very rare in Stoke Heath Borstal. (They probably still would be today, only borstals were abolished back in the Eighties.) So it caused a bit of a stir when a handsome new inmate arrived splendidly attired in light pink overalls. He had left ballet rehearsals at the Opera House Theatre to attend his court hearing believing that, as it was his first offence, he would be let off with a fine. Whether he didn't like pink, or gays, (or both) the magistrate thought otherwise and sentenced him to borstal training.

The young man had a bad time on the prison bus, and it didn't get any easier for him when he came to us. Word soon got around that he was a 'pouf'. (This was way before 'Billy Elliot' put us all straight on that one.) So he was sent outside to work in the canteen out of harm's way.

As a very conscientious dance student he was also concerned about his fitness level for when he returned to ballet school. So I persuaded the P.E.I's to let him train with them in the gym at lunchtime.

One day he came into my office looking grim. He told me he

was fed up with the constant taunting from the others inmates about being a 'pouf', (which he wasn't as it happened, not that it matters).

'I've had it up to here, governor,' he said. 'I've got to do something about it.'

I could see he was very upset so I said, totally against the rules, 'Fine. Do what you feel you have to do. But, remember, we haven't had this conversation.'

The next morning the wing bully, a strapping thug of a youth, was sporting a splendid black eye along with various other cuts and bruises. As it was obvious he had taken a good beating, I asked him if he wanted to press charges against his attacker.

'Nah. It's nuffink like that, governor,' he said very defensively. 'I slipped on the soap in the shower, din't I?'

Inexplicably, our dancer got no more taunting after that.

Shortly before he was due to leave he asked if he could do a performance for the other inmates and, as it would make a welcome break in the prison routine, his request was granted. So he made a music tape of rock and roll hits, created his own routine and practiced religiously over lunchtime. (I wonder, can atheists practice 'religiously?')

As you may know ballet dancing is undoubtedly one of the most physically demanding activities known to humankind. Most forms of dancing require enormous fitness and stamina, but, I'm told, ballet tops them all.

There was an air of expectancy you could have cut with a knife as the other boys took their seats for the performance. When the first bars of the music blasted out and our boy appeared in vest and black tights, (the tights he had borrowed from me as the prison stores were clean out), there were a few amused titters. But by the end of the exhausting and dazzling routine the audience was sitting open-mouthed in admiration. And, as the last sounds of the standing ovation died away, he looked at the audience and said with a grin, 'Now who's a pouf?'

Point well made.

CHAPTER NINE

'Dylan and the Willy on the Wall'

I don't know what it was about me at the time but Prison Service Headquarters seemed to view me as some sort of crusader, or perhaps just a guinea-pig, or more likely, a sacrificial lamb. How else could I explain that, shortly after I joined the service, when female governors were for the first time allowed to work in male prisons, I was the first woman governor to be posted to Stoke Heath Borstal, then to HMP Strangeways and finally to the notorious Dartmoor Jail? Lamb to the slaughter sounds about right.

Male prisons had been bastions of machismo culture since time began. The practices that develop in an all-male environment were well-established, ingrained and fiercely protected. And, of course, the world of the 'funny handshake', freemasonry, with its attendant petty corruption was rife.

It was no secret that the staff at Stoke Heath at first deeply resented a 'split-arse' giving them orders. Their union, the Prison Officers' Association, had even been able to resist matrons who were common in all other borstals. So when, as part of my governor training, I had to go away on courses for a week or so at a time, I would return to find that vital documents I needed for the next management meeting would have somehow gone astray, or be locked in a drawer for which, of course, no one could find a key.

'Sorry, don't know nothing about it, governor.' The attitude was as doubly negative as the grammar.

But by the time my two-year training stint was over and I moved onto Strangeways, I like to think I had won them round. As Bob said, times they were a'changing.

It's an undeniable fact that the introduction of females into male prisons, first as governors and then as officers, changed the culture inside for the better. And vice versa with males being allowed to work in female prisons.

In any potentially explosive incident, and there are several of those in any nick in a day, the dilution of the testosterone levels by a bit of estrogen frequently worked wonders. Irate prisoners eager take on a male officer ('mano-a-mano' as the Spanish say), were often inhibited by the presence of a female. (Though females were sometimes assaulted, of course, as were male officers.) But as a general rule...(Sorry this is beginning to sound like a thesis. I'll get to the rude bits soon.)

The same results occurred in female prisons. Women whose only male role models up to that time had been bullies, drunkards and wasters, responded to the presence of strong but caring, positive male officers. And, despite the previous macho culture, there were a surprising number of that kind around.

'Are you the new governor?'

I was walking across the wing to my new office on my first day at Strangeways, having been out for a liquid lunch with my new boss, the inimitable Norman Brown. Almost his first words on meeting me were, 'Do you take a drink?'

Norman was a legend in the prison service, an ex-tank commander in the Second World War who had been badly burnt when some thoughtless German tossed a hand-grenade inside his tank. I guess after that nothing phased him.

At the time Strangeways was, you could say, a mite overcrowded. Three prisoners to a cell originally designed for one. With no internal sanitation. So, it was understandable I suppose that some of the inmates, rather than share their meager space with a stinking bucket of excrement, would wrap the offending article up and throw the 'shit parcels' out of the window.

Norman was an expert at judging from which cell the parcel had been thrown, and would often be seen gathering them up from the yard, marching onto the wings, opening the culprit's cell door and throwing the parcel back inside along with a pithy comment. It was a sort of a game. And it was better than a hand-grenade, wasn't it?

Norman and I had been first to the bar in the officers' club at lunchtime, where a pint of best was already standing on the bar for him. By the time I had taken a sip of my half pint Norman had drained his glass and another was standing waiting for him.

'I'm happy to join you in drink, sir,' I said with more boldness than I felt, 'but if you don't mind, I'll only pay for one in three.'

Norman laughed and, as the rest of the all-male staff began to fill up the bar, he announced to the room, 'This is the new governor, and she's got more balls than the rest of you put together.'

Norman and I were destined to get on like a house on fire. He was firm but fair, and staff and inmates alike respected and even loved him. They don't make them like him anymore.

But I digress. The questioner was a young officer. "Are you the new governor?'

'Who's asking?' I replied.

'It's just the staff want to know are you a bike or a dyke?'

Made eloquent through drink I replied, 'If I'm a bike the wheel's come off, and if I'm a dyke no man's sticking his finger in my hole, so fuck off!'

Word soon got around not to mess with the new governor.

And word soon got back to me that bets were being taken as to who would be the first to get into the new governor's knickers. It was inevitable, I guess. This was a man's domain and male culture is pretty predictable the world over. But it was one I had to confront if my working life at Strangeways was going to be bearable.

Marching down to the bar I demanded of the barman to see the book.

'Book, governor?' he replied, all innocence.

'There's a book behind the bar with odds on who will be first into my knickers.'

He looked shocked and shook his head. 'Nah. Someone's been

winding you up, governor. There's no book.'

Tired of being pissed about I strode behind the bar, located the book and read it. Then I laughed out loud. The barman frowned, puzzled.

'Too late,' I said, 'it's already happened and his name's not on the list!'

And waltzed out, leaving the barman to ponder the truth or otherwise of that statement. 'Keep 'em guessing.' That's my motto.

The staff didn't take the 'battle of the sexes' lying down. They responded with their own little ploys, like man-handling me into a silent cell and locking me inside for hours. A test as to whether I would go crying to the governor afterwards. The thought never occurred. Norman would have just laughed at me if I had. But there was a battle to be fought and won.

A recent edition of 'PlayGirl' featured a double-page centrefold of a lounging, totally naked hunk sporting what schoolboys used to call a 'lazy lob'. 'Lazy' or not, it was impressive even in that state. (Damian I think his name was, though to be absolutely honest I didn't pay much attention to the words.) My husband hadn't wanted to but I insisted that he go into the newsagent to buy a copy.

The next morning my wing P.O. breezed into my office to give his usual report, stopped dead and stared at the wall behind my head in disbelief.

'You can't have that on the wall, governor,' he said, transfixed by Damian's proud manhood.

'What?' I asked innocently.

'That..That picture.'

I turned to glance at Damian s appendage and turned back.

'Why not?' I replied.

'Well, it's..it's obscene!'

'But it's okay for me to have to go into your offices and have to stare at women's parts every day, is it?' I replied calmly.

It had been the custom for the officers' rooms to be plastered with centrefolds normally reserved for the grimy workshops in garages.

'That's different,' he replied with a trace of uncertainty. This was new territory. Needed careful walking.

'How?' I responded, trying to hide a smile at his obvious discomfort. 'How is it different? It's okay for the young girls from the office to have to look at those pictures, is it? How would you feel if it was your daughter up on the wall, or if she had to look at them every day?'

The P.O. shifted uncomfortably.

'I'll make you a deal,' I went on. 'You get the tits and bums off the walls, and I'll remove the willy.'

He said that he would get the prisoners to remove the photos from their cell walls, but I pointed out that the cells were their living space and the girls from admin didn't go into cells. It was the staff offices that were the problem.

It took a while, but the photographs gradually began to disappear.

CHAPTER TEN

'The Family Fyshe-wycke'

'Governor, governor! I've done it! I've excelled messen this time!' The speaker was Officer Fishwick, the wing character, as he burst into my office one day.

Fishwick was an intelligent man who could have made governor grade, but had chosen to remain a lowly officer all his career. When I asked him why, he explained that as he was the prison photographer and got paid for every mug-shot of every prisoner who came into Strangeways (around 90 per day), he regularly got paid more than the governing governor, but without having the burden of responsibility. It was hard to argue with that logic.

Because he was intelligent prison routine easily bored him so, as officer responsible for cell allocations, he amused himself by trying for unusual groupings of names that he could post on the cell doors. Easy ones were 'Black, Brown and Green' – 'Carpenter, Taylor and Plumber' – 'Long, Short and Shorter'. (You get the picture.)

'I've done it!' he said grinning from ear to ear. 'I've waited years to get this.'

'Go on,' I said. 'Tell me.'

'Freeman, Hardy and Willis!' he announced gleefully. 'I can go to me grave happy now.'

'Fish', as he was known to all, was a bluff Lancastrian with the blunt style of humour typical of that special race. He hadn't a malicious bone in his body, but his remarks could easily be misunderstood by the uninitiated, or the downright thick.

In those grim, grossly overcrowded days prisoners were generally locked in their cells twenty-three hours a day. (Hard to imagine, but its true.) So any time out of cells, however short, was a bonus.

When Fish was on evening duty he regularly unlocked half a dozen Afro-Caribbean prisoners to help serve supper, tea and a bun, to the other cells. It gave them a couple more hours out of their cells, and was a privilege I'm sure they appreciated. So when he would remark to the men lined up, 'Follow me, Oil-slick,' I doubt they took offence.

Not so one passing young governor who, on hearing the remark, told the training department that Officer Fishwick needed to go on a race relations training course. (Get a life!)

The course tutor, a close friend of mine, rang me up towards the end of the course to report that Fishwick had not uttered a single word for four whole days. I remarked that was highly unusual for 'Fish' as normally you couldn't stop him talking.

'What's he up to?' asked my friend.

'I haven't a clue,' I replied. 'But I suspect you're going to find out.'

On the final day, having asked each student in turn what they had got from the course, the tutor turned to 'Fish' and asked the same question.

'Well,' said Fish. 'I think what tha's been trying to say is that it dun't matter what colour a persons' skin is if they were born in Britain they're British.'

'Yes, Mr Fishwick,' said my friend, greatly relieved. 'That's exactly what I've been trying to say.'

'Well that dun't meck no sense to me,' Fish continued. 'I mean if a cat has kittens in a kipper box, it dun't meck 'em bloody kippers, does it?'

Fish used to brag that he could trace his family back beyond Roman times. Challenged to prove his boast he produced a hand-written ancestral chart detailing not only his forebear's names but also their occupations.

Sadly over the years I lost my copy, but my favourites included:

380BC Maximus Fyshwychus
(Toga tugger)

1066AD Elthelred Fyshe-wyke
(Chainmail unraveller)

1135AD Nathaniel ('Splasher') Fyshe-wyke
(Ducking-stool attendant)

1219AD Matilda Fishe-Wicke, Spinster
(Cod-piece upholsterer)

I should add, Officer Fishwick (Prison Jester)

CHAPTER ELEVEN

'It takes all sorts'

In prisons, as in life, tragedy and laughter are never very far apart. Governor to new prisoner in reception, 'And what are you in for?'

Prisoner, 'Battering me wife.'

Custody officer, 'Do you do contract work?'

A youth at Stoke Heath, jailed for savagely beating up his step-father, told one of my officers, 'You know what it's like, sir. I'd been out with me mates. Had a few bevies. I come home and find that bastard has battered me mother and there he was fucking the dog. I just lost it. It could happen to anyone.' (What!)

I was having a break when I overheard the following conversation between two young offenders who were in the wing next to my office.

'Hey, Tommo!'

'What?'

'I'm gonna kill you on exercise!'

Anxious voice. 'What for?'

'None of your fucking business!' (Duh!)

Paddy (an Irishman you will guess) was a 'redband', a prisoner who had more freedom and was given trusted jobs. One day while Paddy was helping the barman stock the shelves behind the bar in the officers' club there was a knock on the door. The club door was next to the main gate so it was easy for a stranger to get confused how to get into the prison.

The barman told Paddy to see who it was. Paddy opened the door to find a delivery man with a parcel in his hand.

'Hey, mate, how do you get in here?' he asked Paddy.

To which Paddy replied, 'I should try a bit of shoplifting. It always works for me.'

Paddy was a Strangeways regular, a harmless petty criminal who had spent most of his life in jail. Like many others, Paddy had become institutionalised and couldn't cope on the outside. Having spent twenty-four consecutive Christmas's in Strangeways, he was looking forward to celebrating his 'silver anniversary' inside when he was told just before Christmas Day that he was due for release. He came to my office in some distress.

'I don't want to go, governor,' he said. 'Where would I go? Who would I spend Christmas with? I don't want to go.'

'I'm sorry, Paddy,' I replied, 'I can't keep you in if you've served your time. It's against the rules.'

Paddy became very agitated. 'But I don't want to go, governor! What can I do?'

'Hit me,' I suggested. 'Then I can take a few days off you and you can stay in.'

Paddy look at me shocked. 'I couldn't do that, Mrs Ellis! I've never hit a woman in me life.'

'Well chuck a brick through a police station window', I joked.

He did. And was back inside for Christmas Eve.

Paddy was family.

The man was an engineer, mid thirties, respectable, married, middleclass, and he was in the prison hospital on suicide watch. Which meant an officer had to check his cell every fifteen minutes because the man, who had just been sentenced to fours years for manslaughter, felt his life was ruined and he was in deep distress.

I had seen him when he came into reception. It was obvious he was not prison material and his state of mind was wretched. He and his wife had been trying for a second child for several years and were delighted when she became pregnant. Sadly their baby daughter was born with a heart defect and spent the first few weeks of her life in hospital in intensive care. When she came out, his mother and father offered to look after the baby and their 8 year old daughter for a night so the couple could go out and celebrate.

They went to a nightclub and on their way out, as the man stopped to talk to the doorman about what a great cabaret they had seen, his wife wandered along the street window shopping. A drunk suddenly appeared and started molesting his wife. The man ran along the street and hit the drunk once. The drunk fell over backwards, hit his head on a lamppost and was instantly killed. The sentence was four years for manslaughter, despite the testimony of the doorman who confirmed the man was only protecting his wife.

He was gradually coming to terms with what had happened when one Saturday morning I got a call to say his baby had been rushed back into hospital with further complications. He went downhill again at that point.

I was also on duty two weeks later when the news came that the baby had recovered and was due to come out of hospital later that day. When I told him he was over the moon.

One hour later I got another phone call and had to go back to his cell again with a very heavy heart. Imagine his horror when I had to tell him the dreadful news that the taxi carrying his wife and baby home from the hospital had been involved in an accident, and that mother and baby had both died. He blamed himself completely as his wife didn't drive and, had he been at home, he would have been driving them.

Such tiny chance moments can change a life forever. In prison you hear of those moments a lot.

In Strangeways remand prisoners, always referred to as 'the innocents', were housed in a separate block. One man who had, allegedly, forced his wife to have sex with an Alsation dog put in an application to see the governor. As I was baby-sitting the unit for a day the man came before me with his complaint, accompanied by the senior officer (S.O.).

He complained that whenever officers opened his cell to take him for exercise they would say, 'Walkies!' And when they let him out for meals the remark unfailingly was, 'Come on Pal, come and get your Chum'.

I turned to the S.O. and said, 'This has got to stop. It's not happening on my watch.'

The S.O. solemnly promised me that it would stop, and that he would personally open the man's cell for the rest of the day.

Later that day the S.O. came into my office, mock-shamefaced.

'I'm sorry, governor,' he said. 'I've let you down.'

'Why's that?' I asked.

'When I opened his cell for his exercise he said to me "I didn't do it, you know. I really didn't do it!".

A gleam came into the S.O.'s eyes as he went on. 'I honestly couldn't help myself, governor. I said to him, I see, it's a case of 'wuff' justice, is it?'

And then there was the one about the flasher. Brought before me having been arrested for flashing outside a home for the blind. This time *I* couldn't help myself.

'I know what you were up to,' I said. 'You were waiting for someone to come along and use the brail method.'

The expression 'All human life is there', I think, sums up the job.

CHAPTER TWELVE

'Do you take a drink?'

All prisons are said to have ghosts. It stands to reason if you think about it. If ghosts do exist, (and I saw a real one in Penstowe Manor years ago) prisons are prime places for them to hang out, if you'll pardon the pun. Especially in the old execution chamber in Pentonville, generally known as 'the topping shed', which was my office for two years. (But more of 'The 'Ville' later.)

It was my first night visit at Strangeways. One of a governor's duties is to make a night inspection from time to time and, on this occasion, I was being escorted along the landings by the newly promoted P.O. The wing was deathly quiet. Our footsteps echoed in the fetid night air. Suddenly we heard it behind us.

'Bloop.'

We stopped and looked at each other. Then looked around. There was nothing but the empty wing. But, as we started to move on..

'Bloop.'

It was soft, but it was definitely there. It was very spooky. Hairs stood up on the backs of our necks. We looked around the landing, searching for the source of the sound.

'Bloop, bloop.'

And there it was right under our noses. As we watched, the lid of the fire bucket hanging on the wall lifted gently and dropped down again.

'Bloop.'

On opening the lid the unmistakable smell of 'hooch' rose to meet us.

'What a shame lads, we've found the still!' I called, my voice echoing around the landing.

Audible groans came from behind many cell doors.

It sounds like a funny story but if someone had tried to put a cell fire out with that bucket there would have been an inferno.

One of my mother's favourite expressions was 'Idle hands make the devil's work,' (usually directed at me as a teenager.) Being locked up twenty-three hours a day leaves prisoners with lots of time on their hands to get up to devilment. From manufacturing weapons out of all kinds of unlikely everyday objects, (razor blades fused into a toothbrush handle is a popular fashion accessory), to making hallucinogenic drugs from the inside of banana skins. But a staple activity is making 'hooch'.

Booze, of a kind, can be made from many things as long as it's organic. Potato skins, fruit, any vegetable matter to hand. But the prime ingredient is yeast. And where do you find yeast? In the prison kitchens. So what is one of the most coveted jobs for a prisoner? (Work it out.)

An ex-inmate of Dartmoor prison, who later became a friend and was one of our wedding guests, tells the celebrated story of 'The Christmas Hooch.'

'I needed constant feeding. Food was always top of my list. Before tobacco, before whackie baccie. So I applied to the kitchen and told them I was an ex army cook. The only job that was going was in the wash up. It was where everyone started and worked up the ranks. So I swung the job.

The kitchen was a mad and wonderful place. It was a huge old kitchen full of cockroaches and villains and bad cooking. One of my fellow inmates there, old Ray, was a chemist and an all round genius! He could get FM radio on the cell bars!! He was full of ideas. One of those was using two sewing needles stuck through the plaster work and into electric cable underneath to power his radio and speakers. Our little gang of nobodies followed suit. We hardly ever had to buy batteries. He also made up a stamp, copied from the Prison stamp for first class post. A rectangle with a small crown in it. This would indicate to the censor that the post was paid for. I wrote many a letter and sent them all over the world, paid for by HMP.

Raymond was a magician. He was able to distill pure alcohol from the yeast I supplied him. He had a still set up in his cell using only a five gallon paint tin and the telescope aerial from an FM radio. (FM radios were banned,)

He had a small veggie oil lamp with which he heated the hooch until it boiled up and then shot out through the telescopic aerial. He poured cold water over it and out dripped the spirit into a tin mug. The still could be dismantled in seconds.

Soon we were running hooch through the nick. Not on a huge scale, litres rather than gallons, but enough to keep a lot of folk happy and keep me in a bit of blow.

Christmas day was coming and we needed lots of Hooch, all the Irish lads wanted a jar. It gets very boring at Xmas. But where the hell to store it? The 'Burglars' search every cockroach infested crack in the whole nick.

The 'Burglars', security screws, made regular snap searches of cells, so cells were ruled out. They also made sweeps of all the other places in the jail, especially the kitchen. It was a real problem. Plenty of nooks and crannies, but they knew them all. Or did they?

As Christmas approached rumors about a stash of booze intended for Christmas Day began to reach the ears of the staff and, soon after, to the cons. All the screws were on the ball! Nothing was getting past them.

The searches continued, leaving no stone or cockroach unturned. It had become a matter of honor for them to thwart the inmates and find the Christmas hooch.

Then one day, while I was working in the kitchen, an eagle-eyed young screw spotted some suspicious looking containers concealed on a shelf way out of reach. Myself and the lads watched with bated breath as the excited search party, who couldn't reach the spoils, dragged a large five gallon metal drum of cooking oil over for the young buck officer to stand on. His first hooch haul. Ah bless him!

Anyway, he jumped up and triumphantly revealed the hidden

containers. Three five litre bottles full of home-made booze. They were only short of dancing! You may imagine we were quite upset.

We took our crest-fallen faces back to our cooking and the screws relaxed and took tea! We could hear their laughter and their cups rattling. They trumpeted their success, and taunted us right up until Xmas day. Cocky bastards!

On Boxing Day, when the staff began unlocking the prisoners cells, they discovered the biggest case of collective hangovers since Woodstock.

And where had we hid the booze? Well I'll tell you. In the feckin' five gallon drums of cooking oil that the big eejit had used to stand on! And if they had looked closer at the three five litre plastic bottles of "hooch" they would have seen it was only apples and water!!'

One up for the prisoners, in what was really a bit of a game that relieved the boredom for everyone.

On the serious side, of course, home-made hooch can be very dangerous. I recall one inmate who had been found with a litre bottle of moonshine beneath his bed. I looked askance at the plastic bottle which had been distorted horribly out of shape by the toxic mix inside it.

'I've a good mind to make you drink it,' I said.

It reminded me of the American TV pharmaceutical adverts, all 'clinically proven' of course, which caution, 'Side effects may include headaches, nausea, dizziness, abdominal cramps, renal discomfort, major organ failure and death.'

Keep taking the tablets.

CHAPTER THIRTEEN

'Busman's holiday'

In the early 1980's San Quentin State Prison was a bleak sandstone castle squatting in a deprived area of the town. Real tumbleweed drifted past the car as we drove up to the gate. The car radio blared the theme from 'The Good, the Bad and the Ugly,' and from the distant mountains smoke signals gave news of our arrival. (No, I made the last two up, but you get the picture.)

My then husband and I were on a three week road trip across the States and the Home Office had arranged for me to visit the infamous jail. I also wanted to visit Disneyland, but my husband said 'No.'

Having parked the car in the car park, we approached the gatehouse which was completely filled by an enormous black woman, a prison guard.

'Don't park yer vehicle there, buddy,' she advised. 'Won't hev no wheels when you cem back.'

My husband re-parked the car at another gate around the side which was manned by a huge guard with a pump-action shotgun. He had planned to stay in the 'vehicle', but decided it might be safer inside with me.

Once inside, on the long walk to the prison itself, we passed an entire fire station inside the walls. Mainly used to quell race riots, we were told.

We were shown in to see the warden, the equivalent of the UK number One governor, who was seated with his leather cowboy boots up on his desk. When he rose he just went up and up and up. We felt like 'limey' hobbits.

We compared notes. At that time Strangeways had about eighteen hundred inmates, his had treble that. (Everything is bigger in America.) He was astounded when I told him there were no guns in our prisons (well, not among the staff anyway.)

'How the Sam Hill do you control the prisoners?' he asked.

'We talk to them,' I replied.

'Shit, my staff don't have the brains to control themselves!' (If he didn t actually say that he implied it.)

His staff were divided into two distinct groups. The unarmed correctional officers who worked inside the prison and the guards on the gantries high up on the prison walls, armed with enough firepower to restart the Iraq War. (Thank you, George, for screwing the world up!)

The warden had trouble recruiting staff and, though he could do a local police check for applicants, the federal check took up to six months. So multiple murderers wanted in another state could walk the gantries armed to the teeth. The officer showing us around told us that the gantry guards had strict instructions in the case of a disturbance, or an attempted escape.

'They hev to fire three shots. One in the air, one in the ground, and one at the prisoner.. But not necessarily in that order,' he added with a grin.

Seeing my expression, he went on, 'Hell, we've had guards killed and hung up round the walls in pieces. You can't take no prisoners in here.' (No irony intended.)

Black, Hispanic and White inmates were kept segregated. Racial violence being one of the prisons biggest problems. As the guard shepherded us through a yard filled with huge black inmates, the wall of prisoners parted to let us through and then closed behind us, and the whistling started. High up on the gantry came the sound of shotguns being primed.

'They're not whistling at me,' I told my husband. 'They're whistling at you.'

'We should have gone to Disneyland,' he said in a strange high voice.

The cages on Death Row were full to the brim. One man, who had been there for twenty years, had been sentenced to 120 years plus death.

'So you're making him the 120 before you kill him,' I quipped. It was a ludicrous sentence. How do you control people with no hope? What do you say to the guy if he writes on the cell wall? 'That's very naughty. Do that again and you'll be in real trouble!'

The elevator on Death Row had doors at either side. One door opened to the exercise yard, the other to the gas chamber. Inside the chamber were two identical chairs, with straps for arms and legs.

'You execute them in pairs?' I asked.

'Sure thing. Haven't you heard there's an energy crisis?'

Apparently, for amusement, the guards sometimes opened the wrong door on purpose. We have gallows humour in our prisons, but there is a limit, isn't there?

I don't know what it's like now, but at that time, I was in no hurry to apply for a transfer to the American system.

CHAPTER FOURTEEN

'Two's company, three's...'

Back in the relative sanity of HMP Strangeways life went on as usual, that is to say you never knew what was going to happen next. Arriving one particular morning I was asked by Norman Brown to investigate an incident that had occurred in a cell on my wing overnight. One of the prisoners, a small, weedy Irishman had been attacked by his cell mate, but was refusing to press charges against his assailant.

I had the Irish inmate brought before me. He had clearly been badly beaten up and didn't want to talk about it.

'T'was just a misunderstanding, governor,' he said nervously, trying to back out the door. 'Just a misunderstanding.'

And that was all he would say. Even when I asked him nicely to go back to his hospital bed and give me a written statement, he had nothing to add.

So I asked for the alleged assailant to be brought up from the segregation unit. When he entered the door the light went out in the room. He was huge.

'I understand there was an incident in your cell last night,' I began.

'Yeah, I hit 'im. I hit 'im. I'm ever so sorry, governor. I wouldn't hurt 'im for the world. He's a nice little geezer.'

I was taken aback. A confession? And I hadn't even got the thumbscrews out yet.

He went on to explain. "See there's three us in the cell, right? There's me on the bottom bunk, the little geezer on the top, and this raving poufter in the single bed opposite.

Well, 'bout 4 o'clock I was sound asleep, right, when the little geezer climbed down from the top bunk to have a Tom Tit. He'd been hanging on, waiting for the pouf to go off, 'cos he din't like dropping his drawers in front of him, see? Well, he did his business and when he got to stand up he slipped and kicked the bucket over. Well, he din't wanna sit down in his own doings, did he? So he grabbed at the first thing he could reach to stop himself.

I woke up. It was pitch black and all I could make out was a geezer with his hand on me leg with his trousers round his ankles. I thought it was the pouf, so I hit 'im.. I'm ever so sorry, governor. Really I am.'

I dismissed the man and, when I'd finished laughing, wrote a report recommending that the Irishman be put back in with the big fella, and that the other inmate should be removed. The report was accepted, with the consequence that the little Irishman had a 'minder' for the rest of his sentence. The big guy was so contrite that he made sure the little chap got his fair share at mealtimes and that no-one ever picked on him.

CHAPTER FIFTEEN

'And now for something completely different.'

Hank Wangford, (you've got to be careful how you say that), is a qualified doctor who mixes the stethoscope with a guitar and has toured the world with his band since the Sixties. Actually called Dr Sam Hutt, his alter ego is an accomplished country singer who writes songs with an ironic, satirical edge, ('Jogging for Jesus, Not Skating with Satan' was his theme song.)

After the success of the TV documentary 'Johnny Cash at San Quentin', Granada Television, based in Manchester, decided to make a home-grown version and approached Strangeways about putting on a concert for the inmates. Muggins was given the job of organizing it, knowing the security department would be having kittens.

Now Strangeways prison at that time had three sections, convicted prisoners, remand prisoners and young offenders. As regulations didn't allow us to mix them, (and we didn't have a space big enough for all who wanted to attend anyway), I told Granada that Hank would have to perform three shows, hoping to get off the hook. Hank agreed.

On the day of the recording they arrived, three huge lorries filled with enough equipment to start a small war.

They had brought their own generator which meant long, thick electrical cables being fed from the street outside into the jail. As the technicians were about to throw the cables over the perimeter wall, I reminded them that this was actually a nick, and that enough prisoners could climb up the cables and get away to confine 'The Great Escape' and Houdini to mere footnotes in the history of escapology. Luckily the cables fitted under the main gate.

The only space large enough for the concert was the chapel and the chaplain had, very reluctantly, agreed to loan it for the event. He instantly regretted his decision as he watched Hank standing in the pulpit with a giant inflatable cactus slowly deflating behind him as he sang 'Big G' with the immortal line 'Drop-kick me Jesus through the goal-posts of Life.'

The first concert was a blast. Everyone, bar the chaplain, loved it. But moments into the second show the generator packed up and all the guitars, amplifiers and speakers went dead. In the deafening silence, two hundred prisoners began to shift in their seats and started to mutter. I had four staff guarding two hundred pissed-off prisoners.

As the muttering grew and the handclaps and foot-stamping were beginning I asked Hank if he could perform without electricity before we had a massive disturbance (several years before the infamous Strangeways riot.) Luckily he had brought along his acoustic guitar and he performed brilliantly with that, like the true professional he is. Phew! And thank you, Hank!

Not wanting to be outdone by their rival company, the local BBC station decided to produce their own 'expose' of life behind bars for the popular radio programme called 'Down Your Way.' And who did they choose as their intrepid reporter? The lovely Pat Phoenix (Elsie Tanner from Coronation Street, for anyone who has never seen one of the most famous soap opera characters in the history of the Universe.)

Now Pat was a brilliant actress and a charming woman, but she had never been inside a prison before and, like most people, was terrified about interviewing prisoners alone. She was very relieved to find that governor Chris Ellis was a woman (people often assumed that a governor called Chris must be a man.) And in the event I had an officer standing by, but out of earshot, so the inmates would feel free to open up to her.

It was an interesting diversion for me, and I got to meet a famous actress who was a delight. Whenever we met shopping in Manchester afterwards Pat and her husband would always stop for a chat. Unlike some stars Pat never got 'above herself' as the Northern expression goes.

All in the day's work of a busy prison governor.

CHAPTER SIXTEEN

'Wire netting and G-strings.'

All good things must come to an end. And so it was with Strangeways. After five memorable and mostly happy years as Governor Five, I passed my promotion interview and moved up the slippery slope to Governor Four. Which meant a new posting as in those days governors weren't promoted in situ.

I took with me many memories. Like the notice from the education department pinned on the wall of the reception room that greeted all new inmates, which read –

'IF YOU ARE ILLITERATE, PLEASE ASK FOR CLASSES.' Priceless.

And the day an officer reported to me that he thought had discovered a secret code word in a prisoner's letters being sent home. This particular inmate was doing time for an armed robbery from which the money had never been recovered, and the police had asked us to pay particular attention to his mail in case there was any clue as to what had happened to the cash.

'He's on about digging in the back garden, governor. It sound like something's hidden there.'

The prisoner was duly sent for and asked to explain the suspicious word. He was a Geordie and not the brightest bulb in the chandelier.

'Why,' he said, 'is that not how ya spell yrnetin?' (Wire netting.)

Talking of prison letters, there is a lovely story told by ex-villain, Dave Courtney, in his autobiography. (A cracking good read, by the way.)

He claims he had been banged up by the Met on a trumped up charge just to get him out of circulation for a while and give the police a breather. He was housed in maximum security prison Belmarsh, inside a prison within a prison where all the really bad boys are put.

One morning, being bored, Courtney walked out of his cell stark naked except for some postage stamps stuck to his forehead. As he lay down on the mail conveyor belt that took the prisoner's letters away an officer asked him what he was doing. To which Courtney replied that he was posting himself back home. On being told to get off the belt and stop fucking about, Courtney replied.

'What's wrong? Haven't I put enough postage on?'

'Do you know the derivation of the word 'fuck'?, I asked one day of an officer who used the word constantly.

'No, governor.'

'It's a legal term from Victorian times,' I lied. 'You know, like TDA stands for 'Taking and Driving Away'. It's an old prostitution charge that stands for 'Felonious Use of Carnal Knowledge.'

'Really governor, I never knew that.'

Months, or maybe years, later when I used the 'f' word on the wing in a moment of exasperation, an officer standing beside me said in all seriousness, 'Do you know the derivation of that word, governor?'

(Yes, you've guessed it.)

Prisons are some of the best places for a laugh, and Strangeways gave me many.

I invited my mother to my leaving do which was held in the prison officer's club. Being a lay preacher she was very interested when a well-built young man entered the packed room dressed as a vicar. Thinking he was the prison chaplain she got up to go over and have a word.

She stopped dead and looked at me as the 'vicar' started removing his clothes. He was the male stripper booked, unbeknown to me, as a special going away treat.

When he got down to his G-string it was time to intervene. Picking him up bodily I propelled him through the emergency doors and into the street, leaving my mother with a very puzzled expression.

Happy days!

Next stop...Dartmoor.

CHAPTER SEVENTEEN

'Drag Queens and Prima Donnas.'

Back where I started ten years ago. The first woman into the notorious Dartmoor Jail, with the prophetic P.O. waiting at the gatehouse to greet me. The media had a field day.

Even before I arrived the grapevine was buzzing. Phone call from Dartmoor security officer to Strangeways counterpart.

'Hey, what's this new governor like? Is she hard?'

'Depends which bit you squeeze,' replied the P.O. 'Ask her yourself, she's standing right beside me.'

Inexplicably the phone line went dead.

My arrival was in all the local papers and the nationals picked it up. I got a call from BBC Bristol asking me to appear on 'Woman's Hour' with the lovely Jeni Murray. Her special guest that day was Danny La Rue, a witty, charming man who insisted on having his photograph taken with me! It was all a bit silly really for a working-class girl from Ashton-Under-Lyne, but it was a giggle.

Another phone call. A television writer in London had seen a photo of me standing at the gates of the prison in the Radio Times. He insisted it would the basis for a cracking TV drama series, and wouldn't take 'no' for an answer.

He wrote three excellent pilot scripts for Yorkshire Television which the producer loved and was convinced would make a long-running series. But the executive producer sat on them until the controller of drama in London persuaded him to front a drama series about a woman prison governor written by Lynda La Plante. Her lame series limped through six episodes and was then not renewed.

But my writer got the best deal. He got me. We've been married eighteen years and counting.

Isn't it strange how things work out? (Never mind, Lynda. Better luck next time.)

Drama seemed to feature a lot during my time at Dartmoor. Finding there was a lack of co-operation and mistrust between the officers and the education and probation department, I persuaded some of them to put on a play together for charity. We wrote a script of 'Allo, Allo' which will never win any Oscars, but I got to play the sexy 'Michelle', the show raised money and people started talking to each other. Job done.

There was also a drama project for inmates being run and filmed by a local film-maker. Don't know what happened to the film, but one of the inmates, our friend of the 'Christmas Hooch' fame, wrote an excellent short play which went on to be performed by the Royal Shakespeare Company at Stratford. That's what prisons should be about. Giving people a second chance. (He was genuinely innocent, by the way.)

Talking of innocence, as in all jails, there was real tragedy and injustice. One of a prison governor's duties is to interview prisoners for parole. And the first question is always to ask if the inmate has come to terms with their offence. That is, are they feeling any remorse or guilt, and understanding of why they did what they were convicted of? If they hadn't there was no way they could be recommended for early release.

Reg Dudley had served ten years of a fifteen year stretch when I first interviewed him for parole. He had been convicted of the infamous 'torso in the Thames' murder, along with another man. His reply to my first question was, 'How can I come to terms with it, governor? I didn't do it.'

Reg was a self-confessed 'fence', not a murderer. He had been convicted through the malice of certain officers of the Met and the blatant lie of a fellow con. He knew that his reply would mean another 'knock-back' for parole, but he wasn't prepared to admit to a crime he didn't commit.

Ten years later he was finally released. In 2002 his conviction for the murder, and that of his 'accomplice', was quashed by the High Court. I hope you got a shed-load of compensation, Reg, for losing twenty years of your life.

Back to the stage. As I said, drama featured a lot at Dartmoor. Shortly before I was promoted again and had to move on, the BBC asked Prison Service Headquarters for permission to film some scenes of the popular soap opera 'Eastenders' in an actual jail. (Fans of the show will remember the time 'Dirty Den' did his 'porridge' inside.) As one of the wings at Dartmoor was being refurbished and had no prisoners the governor asked me if I was happy to 'babysit' the film crew. I agreed on condition that the inmates of the drama group were allowed to watch the filming, out of the way, up on the 'fours' (the fourth landing.) Someone at the Beeb agreed.

The show was conceived and produced by Julia Smith, who regarded herself as the queen of television drama. Julia, who had been known to reduce young girl floor assistants to tears in front of the whole film crew for some minor misdemeanor, was very used to getting her own way.

On the first day of filming some of the off-duty officers stood in as extras for the shoot. As I quietly led my drama group inmates onto the 'fours', way above the actual action, Julia looked up and demanded to know what the hell 'those people' were doing on her set.

'Get those people out of there!' she shouted.

The off-duty staff exchanged looks. They knew what was coming.

'If you don't get out of here at once,' she ranted,
'I will call the governor!'

Leaning over the balcony I calmly projected in my best stage voice, 'I *am* the governor.'

It was a very satisfying feeling.

CHAPTER EIGHTEEN

'Don't show me the way to go home.'

At my promotion interview for Governor Three, in response to many of my replies, one member of the panel invariably asked, 'And what do you think the man on the Clapham omnibus would think of that?'

After the fourth or fifth time I said, 'Remind me never to go to Clapham.'

'Pardon?'

'Well, don t they allow women on buses?'

I passed the interview none the less.

My time at Dartmoor was all too short, but having been promoted I had to move on. I knew I would miss the moor, in all it's seasons (sometimes all four in one day). When sudden snowstorms made it impossible for staff to get home, as it did at least once when I was there, the staff were put up in a barracks type building, while I, as governor, enjoyed the comfort of the village pub's four-poster.

On such occasions the beer in the officers' club was half-price. You can imagine how hard it was for the men, queuing up for the only phone in the club, to inform their wives that they wouldn't be home that night, as the sounds of drunken revelry swelled around them.

'I m really sorry, luv. But we're snowed in. I can't get home.'

Disgruntled voice on the other end. 'Yeah, you sound bleeding sorry. And all your mates in the background singing as well.'

It was during such a bitingly cold spell that I got my first signs of the menopause. Chairing a staff meeting, with snow falling thickly and a biting wind outside, I suddenly began to burn up. (If you've never had a hot flush you wouldn't believe it.)

'Does anyone mind if I open a window?' I asked the assembled men.

'Bleeding hell, governor, it's fucking freezing outside!' was the collective response.

(If men got hot flushes they would have developed an effective remedy centuries ago.)

Every prison has it's Eeyore. The doom and gloom merchant for whom the glass is always half empty.

'Good morning!' I would say cheerily as I walked through the gatehouse, having just had a wonderful drive up from my home in Tavistock to the jail squatting at the top of the bleakly beautiful moor.

'It might be for you,' was his melancholic reply.

On another occasion. "Lovely morning, isn't it?'

'It'll be raining by lunchtime.'

Some people just can't live in the moment, can they, poor souls?

On the night of my leaving do at the officers' club, I was surprised to see 'Eeyore' standing at the bar when I walked in, and I said so.

'Didn't think you'd be here to see me off. Are you here to make sure I really go?'

The reply stunned me. 'No, I'll be really sorry to see you go, governor. You've been a breath of fresh air.'

Blimey O'Reilly, you never know the minute.

It seems some of the rest of the staff felt the same as they'd had a ball and chain made up in the workshop which they put around my ankle. Or that might just have been to stop me getting to the bar.

Though I was sad to leave the jail and my little house in Tavistock, which I had only recently bought, the move maybe saved my life. Or at least saved me and any of my guests from serious injury.

The house was lovely, with a great view of the moor, so I had a buyer within days. But I was astonished when the buyer's survey revealed rampant dry rot. The joists of the lounge were so rotted that as the surveyor said, 'If you'd held a party in the lounge, all your guests would have ended up in the basement.'

It turned out the house was a bank 'snatch-back', bought cheaply by a local builder who had simply built a false wall in the basement to hide the original wall. When that wall was revealed it was riddled with spores that had permeated the rest of the house. I had bought the house through a local agent and solicitor, both of who were apparently in on the scam.

I've locked many people up for lesser crimes than that.

CHAPTER NINETEEN

'And the Oscar goes to...'

On my way to Pentonville Prison in London, I briefly passed through Prison Service Training College, Rugby, a red-bricked, ivy-covered mansion built in the time of Queen Anne. Set in acres of parkland with a lake and black swans, it was quite a contrast to the grim, grey granite of Dartmoor! There I helped train young, wet-behind-the-ears trainee prison officers how to become 'good screws'. Later some of those very students helped me open a new prison on the Isle of Sheppey, and a great job they did too.

The college, with its Italian marble fireplaces and timbered minstrels' gallery, also had a chapel where three years later I had my wedding blessing, presided over by two prison chaplains, both of whom competed to outshine the bride, one in gold brocade and the other in Joseph's coat of many colours. In my career, as often the only woman working in male establishments, I'd been called a 'scarlet woman' many times, so I got married in red.

Pentonville (The Ville) is another grim, grey Victorian nick in the heart of London, and it was there that I had the scariest moment of my career.

Really troublesome prisoners are routinely shipped from one jail to another to give the staff at their permanent jail a breather. A notoriously violent inmate, who regularly assaulted staff, had been sent from Parkhurst Prison for a 28 day 'lie-down'. He had arrived with five officers restraining him, and the orders were that no less than five staff had to be present when he was unlocked. As 'duty dog' I was told that he wanted to see the governor.

'There's no room service at Pentonville,' I said. 'I'll see him when I do my afternoon rounds.'

When I arrived at his cell in the punishment block he said that he wanted to see a proper governor, not a 'split-arse'. (Nice man.)

On being told that he could take it or leave it, he stared at me coldly and said, 'I know you. You've got a daughter called Nancy... And I know where she lives.'

I tried to keep my expression calm, but my blood ran cold. I knew that this was a regular threat made to staff by IRA prisoners in the Maze Prison in Belfast, but it was first time I had encountered it.

The IRA, of course, did have people outside of prison who could carry out their threats. Did this inmate as well?

I didn't know.

With a calmness I certainly wasn't feeling, I replied, 'What do you want, a round of applause?'

It was an Oscar-winning performance, but when I left his cell my legs were shaking. Not for myself. But for what could happen that I could do nothing about. In the event the police were asked to do extra patrols in the vicinity of my daughter's house, and to respond immediately if they got a call from her. Thankfully, it proved to be an empty threat, as most are.

Another situation, which this time left my new husband, the writer, shaken, was the Yardie who, having seen me from behind wearing black stockings, was convinced I was really a black woman. He fell in lust and vowed, on his release, to kidnap me and take me back to Jamaica.

I had moved on from 'The Ville' by the time he was let out, but when we heard the news of his release my husband kept a baseball bat by the front door for several weeks afterwards.

Talk about bringing your work home!

CHAPTER TWENTY

'There's no business like show business.'

I don't know what it is about me but, in my career as a governor, the world of entertainment seemed to follow me around. Hank and Pat at Strangeways, 'Allo Allo' and Eastenders at Dartmoor.

Pentonville - Status Quo and Esther Rantzen!

I have always believed that the main purpose of prison is rehabilitation. What's the point of locking someone away and not giving them any skills to try to change their way of life when they get out?

Now I know the newly privatised prisons in the UK don't share that view. But be fair, they are about maximizing profits and the more times an offender returns to them the louder the cash register rings somewhere in corporate America.

'Come back soon, y'all! We'll keep yer bunk warm fer ya!' (There must be some Texans in the mix somewhere. They even let one into the White House, God help us!)

However, the credo of the UK prison service has always been about returning offenders to the outside world better fitted to cope with life. So when, as governor in charge of inmate activities, I was given the opportunity to help set up a job club in Pentonville I threw myself into the project wholeheartedly.

Raising money finding space, begging and borrowing equipment (I'll leave out the 'stealing'), we were able to give offenders nearing the end of their sentence career advice, interview training and real job opportunities. Potential employers were invited into the prison to interview inmates for existing positions in their companies. Bank staff came in to advise prisoners who wanted to set up their own businesses on the outside. It was one of the best times for me in the service, and I was very proud of our successes.

Alongside the job club, activities for inmates flourished. The most notable being the rock band set up by P.I.E. Doug Jackson. Begging equipment and musical expertise from outsiders, (like my husband's son-in-law who was performing in 'Buddy' in the West End at that time), Dougie created a group of musicians that could have rocked many venues.

His crowning coup was persuading the super duo Status Quo to come into the jail to give support and advice to the inmate performers. I was there as the new band performed a concert for the inmates with Status Quo in the audience. It was a magical moment. 'Jailhouse Rock' for real.

Unknown to Dougie the members of the prison band wrote to Esther Rantzen, who at that time was hosting a very popular BBC television show called 'Hearts of Gold'. The premise of the show was for members of the public to nominate people who had done selfless and remarkable things for a 'Hearts of Gold' award. The band members nominated Doug and, unsurprisingly, he was chosen.

A few days prior to the recording at Television Centre Esther and a film crew arrived at Pentonville to film material for the show. They wanted to interview, not only the band members, but also members of staff, including myself as governor in charge of activities.

On the morning of the filming, while eating an apple for breakfast, I broke one of the two crowns in the front of my mouth. Not a pretty sight. The prospect of being filmed for national television with a fang hanging down like Dracula wasn't appealing. And, as a hopeless ventriloquist, I knew I couldn't get away with talking with my mouth closed. I stuck the crown back in with chewing gum and, unable to get a dental appointment at such short notice, I hurried to the prison dentist. Several inmates were sitting patiently waiting their turn.

'I'm sorry, guys,' I began, 'I wouldn't normally pull rank but this is an emergency.'

To illustrate my dilemma I removed the crown and smiled. To a man they recoiled.

'God, governor, go in!' they cried. 'You need it more than us!'

Sadly, after I left The Ville a new breed of reactionary Tory Home Secretary came to power, and the job club, along with many other enlightened initiatives for inmates, died. 'Hearts of Gold?' I don't think so.

CHAPTER TWENTY-ONE

'Mrs Thatcher's Recipe Book.'

Ingredients - Take 1,647 prisoners in a jail designed to hold 970, lock them up three to a cell 22 hours a day, seven days a week, sharing a bucket as a toilet. Result – The Strangeways Riot.

That recipe got me talking to BBC presenter, John Humphries, from a radio car outside my house at seven in the morning wearing my dressing gown and slippers (I didn't have my hair in curlers as it naturally looks 'afro'.) As assistant general secretary for the Prison Governors' Association (PGA) it was my role to field questions about the riot for the radio. The general secretary, Lynne Bowles, drew the short straw. She did the television interviews and had to dress up to appear before the cameras for the morning Sky News programme til the late night grilling by Jeremy Paxman on 'Newsnight'. While I could sit with my feet up with no make-up, nursing a cup of coffee and smoking a fag, chatting over the air waves with nice Mr. Humphries.

In the event Lynne and I spent a lot of our time defending our PGA chairman from misinformation fed to the press from a Teflon-shouldered Home Office, who were anxious to shift the blame and discredit our embryonic organisation. Hey, can you blame them? The PGA was effectively a trade union, and those things were evil, weren't they? Conveniently for the Home Secretary, Mr Waddington (who should have stuck to making games), our chairman was Brendan O'Friel, the governor of Strangeways Prison.

On April 1st 1990 when Brendan O'Friel got a phone call to say there was a full-scale riot at his prison it's reported that at first he thought it was an April Fool's prank. Twenty five days later Strangeways lay in ruins and 147 officers had been injured.

All prison staff know that jails are run with the tacit cooperation of the inmates. At any given time prisoners far outnumber the officers guarding them so a degree of grudging respect has to exist for things to go smoothly. But when conditions for both inmates and staff are really bad that respect and co-operation breaks down.

In the Thatcher mania for public service cost-cutting prisons had been first in line. Fed on a diet of lies and half-truths by the tabloid press the general public thought all jails were holiday camps, so they were an easy target for the 'slash and burn' mentality current at that time.

Brendan O'Friel had warned the Home Office many times over many months that unless he was given extra resources he would be unable to 'keep the lid on' his jail indefinitely. His warnings went unheeded.

Result? 55 millions pounds to rebuild the shattered jail and much more spent pensioning off severely traumatized staff unable to return to work.

Great house-keeping Mrs T!

CHAPTER TWENTY-TWO

'A dream is a wish your heart makes.'

After years of working in the grim confines of Victorian jails, leaving my pokey office at The Ville to open a brand-new, squeaky-clean prison was one of the highlights of my career. Elmley prison on the Isle of Sheppey at the mouth of the River Thames had just been completed, and even before the paint was dry I moved in as deputy governor. My new boss, John Cooper, a highly intelligent, caring man, had a vision of what a 20th century prison should be like.

'I have a dream,' he said to me at our first meeting. (Bit like Martin Luther King.) 'And I want you to make it happen.'

To say I was chuffed was an understatement. John and I shared the same values. I was being given the chance to be part of establishing a new regime with 80% of the staff straight from basic training, not hardened old-timers with outdated, ingrained practices. The opportunity to put into practice all the positive things I had learnt over the years from the great people I had worked with was a privilege not granted to many governors.

The problems started from day one. Elmley was empty. Not just of inmates, but equipment. Everything had to be shipped from the stores in Corby. Beds, shelves for the kitchen ovens, you name it. No problem you would think. But there are three prisons on Sheppey. All within spitting distance of each other.

So where does our consignment of beds go? Swaleside, the prison next door.

'Not ours, mate,' said the Swaleside stores officer. 'We've got beds.' Neglecting to mention that next door Elmley prison was brand-spanking new and probably needed some beds. So naturally the beds were driven back to Corby.

However, the shelves for the ovens did arrive on time. But they were the wrong size and couldn't be made to fit no matter how we tried. Back to Corby. If you want something really screwed up ask a civil servant.

And so it went on, two steps forward one back, with the deadline for taking our first batch of prisoners fast approaching. At that time police cells were overflowing with prisoners who should have been in prison, so the pressure from head office for us to get up and running was immense. They'd have had us open without beds or ovens if they could have got away with it.

Convicts can be wily and devious. Let's face it they have all day to think up schemes to frustrate and hoodwink prison staff. So along with the 'virgin' officers straight from training college it was necessary to bring in a tier of middle management, principal and senior officers, who had been around the block a few times, but hadn't become jaded and cynical.

I was delighted when two reception staff from Pentonville volunteered to join the team to set up the operating systems. They relished the chance to establish a new, unique tone for the embryonic prison.

They put a 'Welcome' mat at the door of the reception room, and the first thing a new prisoner saw on entering was an oven glove, with a face drawn on it, peeping above the desk saying, 'Welcome to HMP Elmley. Would you like double or single, smoking or non-smoking, tea or coffee in the morning, and what time would your like your alarm call?'

Some of the old lags were a bit taken aback at first, but it set the attitude for the whole jail.

Like the case of the missing teddy bear. One Governor Five was a macho man, an ex-P.E.I (physical education instructor) who spent all his spare time pumping iron in the gym. Then one day a member of staff noticed something strange nestling in the governor's kitbag. It was a tiny teddy bear. And too good a chance to pass up.

'Who's nicked my fucking teddy bear?' I heard echoing down the wing one day after lunch.

He stormed round the wing searching everywhere. A bear of a man, searching for his little friend. But the bear kept eluding him. Even the prisoners were in on it, and passed the bear around their cells as he became more and more ballistic.

A ransom note appeared. 'Pay up or the bear gets it.'

Eventually Daddy Bear and Baby Bear were reunited. And he took it in good part really. It was all part of the feeling of the jail.

With everyone pulling together in the same direction, Elmley became the brightest, happiest jail I have ever worked in, for staff and inmates alike. John Cooper's dream had come true.

CHAPTER TWENTY-THREE

'There's more ways than one...'

Not everyone plays by the book. During my time most governors I knew were individuals not civil service robots. Mavericks sometimes, always sharp, life-skilled people who did it their own way, when they could get away with it. And if they couldn't, well, they did it anyway.

My personal mentor, Peter Pope, was famous for cutting his nose off to spite his face if he felt he had to speak out against Home Office pomposity, absurdity and sheer bone-headedness. (And there was plenty of that!)

Peter was due to give the wind-up speech at one conference where 'experts' had spent many hours lecturing governors about a new I.T. system which the mandarins at head quarters had dreamt up. (Maybe if they were given some proper work to do they wouldn't have time to sit around dreaming up hair-brained, half-assed initiatives!) [Did you notice I'm prejudiced against civil service mentality?]

Anyway, back to the conference. Striding to the podium Peter put his forefinger onto the small projection screen of the overhead projector. The image of his pinky loomed large on the big screen behind him.

'I believe I'm right in saying that is a digital readout,' he said.

He continued deadpan, as he began to write on the screen, 'To sum up I think what we have been learning here today is -
Systems **H**i-tech **I**nformation **T**echnology.'

Home Secretary Willie Whitelaw, when visiting Peter's office at Dorchester Prison, was surprised to see a photograph of Hitler on the opposite wall to a portrait of Winston Churchill. On being asked the reason for the unusual juxtaposition of the two photos, Peter replied that he believed in always taking a 'balanced' view.

Having been forewarned of the kind of man he was dealing with, as a wily politician Whitelaw should have been canny enough not to ask why Peter had framed all his many promotion rejection slips and hung them on the wall behind his desk.

'Ah, that's just to remind me,' said Peter, 'that shit always floats to the top.'

Needless to say Peter never got the promotion he was due.

As you will have gathered, in those days every governor had their own individual style. Mine was based on humour and natural cunning. The humour from my dad, the cunning from my mother. (She once persuaded my dad not to cast his Labour vote as it would only be cancelled out by her voting Tory. Then, while he was sleeping in the armchair after an unusually stodgy meal she had cooked, my mother crept out and voted for her beloved Conservatives.)

Inmates sometimes barricade themselves in their cells. (I never quite understood why since they were locked in anyway.) The standard practice, after all persuasion had failed, was to take the door off, rush in mob-handed and take the prisoner down to the punishment block. But that was messy and could result in the inmate and officers getting hurt.

One particular female, a sad case already in the punishment block, had been barricaded in her cell for hours and refused to come out. Why not leave her in, you might say? But that often led to the prisoner damaging the cell or themselves and, as officer in charge, I was held responsible for both.

Knowing this particular individual loved her food, I sent word to the kitchen to fry up some bacon and have it sent to the wing. The plate duly arrived and within minutes of wafting the beautifully crisp, aromatic bacon outside her cell door she was pleading to be let out. I made her wait until I was good and ready.

It was an unusually sunny day at Pentonville when a group of prisoners on exercise decided that they would prefer to stay in the sunshine rather than return to their cosy cells. That was a problem because other inmates were waiting to come out for their exercise, and were beginning to get restless. (Any disruption of routine in prisons can cause a disturbance.)

I had twelve staff supervising over a hundred prisoners. Not good odds for manhandling the reluctant inmates back inside. That could have turned very unpleasant and, as a naturally happy person, I can't stand unpleasantness. But I had a lot of restless prisoners inside waiting for their turn in the sun. You've heard the phrase 'Between a rock and a hard place.'?

As the sun burned down and the lounging inmates began to bake, I asked the kitchen to send up twelve portions of peaches and cream. To hell with the budget, lots of cream!

The brimming bowls arrived and were handed out to the twelve officers on duty in the yard. I didn't have to tell them to relish it. They knew. There were several Oscar-winning performances of lip-smacking and appreciative grunts. Disgruntled murmurs began to rise from the sunbathers. (Not surprisingly, being banged up most of the day in tiny, smelly cells, food is one of the major issues for inmates in jails. Mealtimes can sometimes take on an almost religious aura, or be like feeding time at the zoo.)

An inmate strode up to one of the officers and said, 'This is psychological harassment.'

On hearing this I said, 'If he can say psychological he must be one of the ringleaders.'

One by one, then in small groups, the prisoners meekly asked to let back inside. The ringleaders were made to wait til the last.

TWENTY-FOUR

'Does she take sugar?'

I forgot to mention that during my time as tutor at the prison service college in Rugby I was sent to train a group of new recruits at the newly built prison on the island of Guernsey. (What a cushy number I hear you say.)

The old prison was a castle so tiny that officers didn't need radios to communicate, they could shout from one side to the other. So one of the first things my colleague, Mick Roebuck, and I had to do was teach the new officers the use of radios in jail. Except, courtesy of the civil servants, there were no radios. They were no doubt still sitting on a shelf in Corby, or being ferried to various parts of the country to jails that didn't need them. Being highly-skilled senior management, trained to think on our feet, we improvised using fag packets and had officers walking round the jail talking into packets of Benson and Hedges and Silk Cut. But you don't get the range or sound quality with them. We would have been better off with two tin cans attached with string.

On our first day I was offered a cup of tea in the staff-room.

'Do you take sugar, governor?' I was asked.

'No, thanks,' I replied.

'That's good, you can never find a teaspoon in this place.'

I went to the governor and asked him how long he'd had a drug problem in the prison.

He frowned. 'We don't have a drug problem.'

'Believe me if you keep losing teaspoons, you have a problem. Someone is chasing the dragon.'

On our next trip back from the UK to the island Mick and I were armed with the official drugs teaching kit. A briefcase full of Class A and B drugs. (We collected it ourselves. Certainly couldn't trust the civil service with that!)

Late for the plane at Heathrow we were racing through security when we were stopped for a random search.

'We're going to miss our plane!' I cried.

'Just open the briefcase, please.'

While I frantically rummaged through my handbag for the briefcase key, Mick was trying to find the Home Office letter authorizing our possession of the illegal drugs.

'What's in the briefcase?' the security officer asked, watching our frantic efforts.

In for a penny I thought, took a deep breath and said, 'Heroin, crack cocaine, marijuana, LSD, amphetamines..'

The officer looked at me for a moment as I emptied the contents of my handbag onto his counter.

'Go on, off you go,' he said with a wave of his hand. 'No one would make that up.'

Mick was a passionate fly-fisherman and was brilliant at making his own 'flies'. They are the bait fly-fishers use, bits of different coloured feathers tied together, each crafted for a particular type of fish, and each one a tiny work of art in itself.

I have never caught a fish in my life, but I became fascinated with the process and asked Mick to show me how to make a fly. (Believe me evenings in Guernsey can be pretty dull.) I enjoyed it and was quite proud of my efforts. But I made the cardinal mistake. I told my class of young officers.

'Did you have a good time last night, governor, playing with Mr Roebuck's flies?' was the morning greeting.

I should have known better.

CHAPTER TWENTY-FIVE

'The beginning of the end.'

Cookham Wood in Kent was a women's prison that had never had a female governor. Amid rumours of problems with the female staff I was appointed governor in charge. My first (and last) posting as top dog.

While it was gratifying to be given my own jail with an 11 million pound budget, I knew that if anything went wrong it was my head on the block. This was at a time when the prison service was beginning to turn away from the progressive reforms briefly implemented after the Woolf report which followed the Strangeways riot, towards a 'blame' culture with politicians interfering in operational decisions, which they were not supposed to do. (Try telling a politician anything they don't want to know.)

As assistant general secretary for the PGA, I had recently represented two of my governor colleagues at disciplinary hearings, so I knew that the knives were out for governors, and that the tabloid press were being fed lies and half-truths to 'scapegoat' individuals rather than the prison service management. So, it was not without misgivings that I stepped over the threshold of Cookham Wood. (Not without foundation as it turned out.)

My experience as a basic grade officer at the start of my career, many years ago, stood me in good stead. In all work places there are 'Spanish practices'. (Having lived in Spain for over a decade I now understand the meaning of that phrase!)

Cookham was no exception. My first action was to ask to see the duty rosta.

The senior officer who was in charge of allocating duties and shifts for all the staff replied, 'Oh, you don't want to bother yourself with those little details, governor.'

Oh, but I did. And discovered, as I had suspected, that there were 'favourites' in the pecking order. Some staff being given easy duties and favourable shift patterns, while others got the anti-social hours and the crap duties.

An unrecognized power structure existed in the jail that had little to do with rank and more to do with the 'witches coven', as it was known. There was a large eye painted in the wall of the male toilets, for what purpose I never discovered, and stories of chicken bones being left outside cell doors to frighten the occupants. A lot of the inmates were drug 'mules' from African villages who believed in witchcraft and black magic, and that sort of thing terrified them as some members of staff well knew.

The 'mules' were generally simple peasant women who had been threatened, or blackmailed with threats against their children, into smuggling small quantities of drugs into the UK as a decoy. An anonymous tip-off to the authorities resulted in the 'mules' being caught, while the bigger drug consignment on the same plane went through undetected.

It was heart-breaking to see these duped women locked up for years, thousands of miles away from their children.

Gradually, by winning the confidence of some of the stronger staff members, who were opposed to the unofficial power structure but had no power to confront it, myself and my deputy, Carol, managed to eliminate most (I'm sure not all) of the injustices within the prison.

The biggest injustice of all, though, I had no power to control. Because it came direct from the Home Office.

CHAPTER TWENTY-SIX

'Head's they win, tales I lose.'

Throughout my time as a prison governor my mother was always on at me to get a 'proper job'. But secretly I think she was proud of my career. She had visited me in most of my postings, and was very keen to visit the prison of which her baby daughter was in charge.

She had put on her 'Sunday best' and was seated in my office when my 'tea-lady', a slim woman in her mid-forties with short dark hair, brought in the tray.

'Here you are, Mrs Roberts,' she said, handing my mother a china cup.

'A china cup!' I exclaimed. 'What's wrong with the mugs?'

'You can't give your mother tea in a mug!' was the shocked reply. 'And I've brought you some rich tea biscuits, Mrs Roberts.'

I could see my mother was enjoying being treated as 'royalty'. The governor's mother.

'Thank you, Myra,' I said as the woman left with the tray.

'Myra?' my mother asked as the door closed.

'Yes, Myra Hindley. Myra's my tea-lady.'

My mother stared at the untouched teacup with alarm. 'I'm not drinking that,' she said. 'She might have poisoned it!'

Bless her, my mother's reaction was typical of almost the entire population of Britain. I couldn't blame her. Fed a diet of half-truths, lies and more lies by the tabloids, led by Murdoch's rag 'The Sun', Myra had been demonized like no other prisoner before, or probably since.

Knowing that Cookham Wood housed Britain's most notorious female prisoner, reporters constantly door-stepped staff, looking for juicy bits of gossip that they could blow up and exaggerate for their front pages.

Some of the 'Myra' stories could only have come from the 'lifer' section at headquarters. Like the news that, though she had served many more years than her recommended tariff, Myra had been told that she would never be released. I was the person given the unenviable task of giving her that news.

A prisoner's 'tariff' is the number of years recommended by the trial judge that an offender should serve in prison. Now in our country politician's are not supposed to have any say in judicial decisions, but in the case of Myra successive Home Secretaries, scared of the public's reaction whipped up by the tabloids, treated her as a separate case and ignored the judicial process afforded to all other prisoners.

I hold no brief for what Myra did. But even the Krays were allowed to attend their mother's funeral. Terrified of the press reaction, The Home Office denied Myra the right to see her dying mother, or even to go to her funeral. And yet there were many who had committed worse crimes who had served their time, been released and were walking the streets. Throughout my time as her governor, I learnt that there was one law for Myra, and another for everyone else. In any civilized society's book that's not right, is it?

In those days governors worked 10 days on and 4 days off, and on my 10th day on duty, my Deputy rang to say she was sick and couldn't cover for me the next day when I was due to be off work. So I stayed on duty the next day until I could arrange for cover from the 3rd in charge Governor.

Unknown to me, (as I was not supposed to be on duty and anything to do with Myra was on a 'need to know' basis), Myra had a hospital appointment that day. Although the security department would normally have dealt with the matter without my help, the prison van broke down and they sensibly didn't want to get a taxi in case the driver got wind of the fact it was Myra and tipped off the press.

I was due to leave for home after lunch so I agreed to take the two staff (in civvies) and Myra to the hospital in my car, wait until she was finished, then drop them back at the prison before driving home to London.

Myra had a regular appointment for a heart condition and always went under an assumed name. What we didn't know was that during a visit to the prison some months earlier, a journalist had somehow found out about the hospital visits and had bribed someone at the hospital to tip her off when the next appointment was due under that assumed name.

Seated in the waiting room chatting with Myra I noticed a young man reading a newspaper who occasionally glanced over at us. As I was a bit 'hot' in those days, I thought nothing of this male attention. (That's a joke, folks!)

When I arrived home in Muswell Hill that evening my husband was waiting at the door holding out a glass of red wine.

'Here,' he said. 'Drink that. You're going to need it.'

The prison service had been on the phone, he told me, wanting to talk to me about a front page newspaper article, due to be published next day, complete with a photo of my car, reporting Myra's hospital visit and a 'verbatim' record of our conversation in the waiting room.

'Verbatim' except that, as Myra had been out of Manchester much longer than I, the reporter had mistaken my Northern accent for hers, and had completely reversed the conversation, putting my words in Myra's mouth and mine in hers. Not that it mattered as it was only small-talk, but it just goes to prove you should never believe everything you read in the papers, except the date.

The result? I arrived at my car a few days later to find the driver's door kicked in. The newspaper hadn't bothered to blank out the number plate on my car. Deliberate? Who knows? After what's been revealed over the recent Murdoch affair you can be excused for believing the press are capable of anything.

Adding insult to injury, headquarters initiated an investigation into my conduct, affectively accusing me of colluding with the media! (Me, who wouldn't piss on a tabloid reporter if they were on fire!) But, by then, the Home Office 'blame' culture had really taken hold and I was only one of many of my fellow governors under investigation.

It was calculated that around that time every governor in the prison service was either being investigated for misconduct, or was conducting an investigation into one of their own colleagues. What a sad waste of talented people and tax-payer's money, all because people at the top wanted to divert attention from themselves and cover their asses!

(Did I mention I don't like the civil service culture?)

EPILOGUE

'The moving fingers writes, and having writ moves on.'

I had been in the prison service almost twenty years when headquarters brought out an initiative granting early retirement at fifty to any eligible governors. I believe almost all of them applied, which speaks volumes for the state the prison service was in.

Peter Pope, of Hitler versus Churchill fame, had long gone, having refused to sign a contract that could penalize governors, but which had no penalties for the prison service if it did not keep to its side of the contract.

John Marriot, a talented, inspirational man, known as 'the governor's governor', had been hounded out of the service when Michael Howard announced in Parliament that John would never be allowed to govern a prison again after three prisoners escaped from Parkhurst on the Isle of Wight. This despite the fact that historically politicians had never interfered in operational matters, and that John had for months sent repeated requests to head office for technical equipment to prevent such an escape. (The prison was under refurbishment at the time and had been described as 'a sieve.)

The writing was on the wall. All the 'mavericks', the talented, individualistic, experienced people who had contributed so much to the service over the years were bailing out.

It was time to go. I'd had a great time working in prisons and met many wonderful people, both staff and inmates alike. But it was no longer the service I had grown to love and care about. Politics, not the inmates, had taken over the institution.

Today there are twice as many prisoners in British jails than when I started as a lowly officer. Until a government comes along that believes prisons are for rehabilitation as well as punishment I suspect the number will continue to rise. And then one day someone will decide that the burden is too much for the taxpayer and privatise the whole shebang. To the great delight of the American shareholders of our privatized prisons.

'Keep 'em coming, bubba!' I hear them cry.

A young lad who had been kicked out of every borstal for bad behaviour arrived at Stoke Heath and was sent straight to the punishment block. As it was my job to check on prisoners before I went off duty, I went into the boy's cell, sat down on his bed and said, 'Okay. Bedtime. Which fairy story do you want?'

The lad stared at me, wide-eyed, then called to the officer standing at the door, 'Get her out of here! She's mad!'

Well, maybe...But maybe if someone had read him bedtime stories when he was a kid he wouldn't have been in there in the first place.

Also by Harry Duffin

Chicago May

In 1919, stealing money to escape a violent, abusive father, sixteen year old May Sharpe flees her native Ireland to chase her dream of finding a new life in America. But, arriving penniless in New York, May has to make a stark choice, between living an honest life in poverty, or crime.

Within two short years., May becomes the toast of the city's criminal community. But, at the hight of her success, May is forced to re-examine her morality, and loyalties, and make a decision which could threaten, not only her new-found fame and fortune, her young life.

Inspired by a true story.
Available on Amazon Books.